STATE TAXATION OF BANKS

STATE TAXATION
OF BANKS

By

JOHN BROOKS WOOSLEY

PROFESSOR OF ECONOMICS
UNIVERSITY OF NORTH CAROLINA

CHAPEL HILL
THE UNIVERSITY OF NORTH CAROLINA PRESS
1935

PRINTED AND BOUND IN THE UNITED STATES OF AMERICA
BY THE SEEMAN PRINTERY, INC., DURHAM, NORTH CAROLINA

THIS BOOK WAS DIGITALLY PRINTED.

PREFACE

FOR some fourteen years the legal status of the state taxation of banks, never too definitive, has been very precarious. Most states during this period have encountered unusual difficulties in imposing legally valid levies on national banks, and in numerous instances they have been equally limited in the taxation of banks of their own creation. Not only have state and local governments suffered substantial losses in revenue from bank tax invalidations, but the immediate and future status of income taxation and the classified property tax are also inextricably involved in the bank tax problem. This study traces the evolution and implications of the legal issues which revolve around the taxation of banks, and evaluates the methods of bank taxation now in force in the several states. A suggested solution of present difficulties is offered for such consideration as its merits may warrant.

An exploration of the problem of bank taxation was first suggested to me by Professor Jacob Viner of the University of Chicago. The study, of which this monograph is a summary, was later pursued under the generous and stimulating direction of Professor Simeon E. Leland, of the same university, to whom I am most deeply indebted for his sustained, critical interest at all stages of its progress. I am under obligation to Professors Arthur H. Kent and L. W. Mints, also of the University of Chicago, for their suggestions relating, respectively, to certain constitutional and banking aspects of the problem. Mr. Martin Saxe, of Morris, Plante and Saxe, New York City, and Mr. W. H. Blodgett, formerly Commissioner of Taxation in Connecticut, read the original manuscript and offered several suggestions as did also my colleague, Professor H. D. Wolf. The unstinted aid of my wife has been invaluable in the prosecution of the study.

Notwithstanding the liberal assistance received from these sources, errors of fact and interpretation may remain for which I am wholly responsible.

JOHN B. WOOSLEY

Chapel Hill, N. C.
June, 1935

CONTENTS

                                                            PAGE

PREFACE... v

CHAPTER

I. THE PROBLEM OF NATIONAL BANK TAXATION.......... 3

II. STATUTORY EVOLUTION OF SECTION 5219, 1864-1923..... 9

III. THE INTERPRETATION OF SECTION 5219 BY THE
      UNITED STATES SUPREME COURT.................. 19

IV. THE AMENDMENTS OF 1923 AND 1926 TO SECTION 5219.. 53

V. THE MOVEMENT FOR THE FURTHER AMENDMENT
     OF SECTION 5219............................... 66

VI. INCOME AND EXCISE TAXATION OF BANKS.............. 80

VII. THE TAXATION OF BANK SHARES AT GENERAL
      PROPERTY RATES............................... 91

VIII. THE UNIFORM RATE ON BANK SHARES................ 111

IX. THE DISPROPORTIONATE TAXATION OF STATE BANKS.... 120

X. A SUGGESTED SOLUTION FOR THE BANK TAX PROBLEM... 125

APPENDIX 132

STATE TAXATION OF BANKS

CHAPTER I

THE PROBLEM OF NATIONAL BANK TAXATION

THE absence of a single homogeneous banking system in the United States has perennially clouded the state tax status of banks in legal uncertainties. The sources of many of these issues are to be found in our dual system of government and our multiple banking organizations. A banking system is maintained by each of the several states and by the federal government. State banks are chartered by the state and operate under the state banking code. The national banking system is a creature of the federal government and its members function under federal law. As federal agencies, national banks enjoy certain legal immunities with respect to state taxation that state banks are not always in a position to demand. The limitations which surround the states in the taxation of national banks have their judicial genesis in the famous decision of Chief Justice Marshall in *McCulloch* v. *Maryland*[1] (1819), which invalidated taxes imposed by Maryland on the Baltimore branch of the Second United States Bank on the ground that the federal government and its necessary agencies, being supreme, were free from the potentially destructive taxation of the several states. This theory was further elaborated in *Osborne* v. *The Bank*[2] to include the activities and operations of the bank.

While the bank, its activities and its operations were declared free from state taxation, the court observed in the former case that the decision did not deprive the state of its original and sovereign powers to tax the real estate owned by the bank or "the interest which the citizens of Maryland may hold in this institu-

[1] *McCulloch* v. *Maryland,* 4 Wheat 316 (1819).
[2] *Osborne* v. *The Bank,* 9 Wheat 738 (1824).

tion." Likewise, in the latter case the court indicated that the "local property" of the bank was taxable by the state. Inferentially, therefore, the real estate and shares of the bank were taxable by the state.

Since the creation of the National Banking System in 1863, statutory enactments by the Congress and their interpretation by the Supreme Court of the United States have combined to limit the power of the states both as to the method and extent of national bank taxation.[3] From 1864 until 1923 the states were permitted to tax national banks on their real property with the further provision that the value of the bank shares might be taxed to the holder, provided the rate imposed on such shares was not higher than the rate imposed "on other moneyed capital in the hands of individual citizens of that state." The tax on the real estate of national banks has rarely constituted a serious load, owing to their small investments in such property, but the tax on their shares frequently has assumed burdensome proportions. While the share tax is nominally imposed on the shareholder, it is in effect levied on and collected from the bank. As the rate to be imposed by the state on the value of national bank shares is restricted to the rate imposed upon "other moneyed capital," the definition of this term by the courts became the crucial limit in the share taxation of national banks.

Through a process of progressive definition the United States Supreme Court in the Richmond case[4] in 1921 unequivocally established the principle that national bank shares could not be taxed at a higher rate than was imposed on other competing moneyed capital in the hands of individuals, and that such competing moneyed capital included bonds, mortgages, notes and credits held merely as private investments if such holdings were

[3] See chaps. 2-3, *infra*.
[4] *Merchants' National Bank of Richmond* v. *City of Richmond*, 256 U. S. 635 (1921).

substantial in amount. Though this position had been clearly indicated by the court in prior decisions, neither the tax officials nor
the state legislatures had been fully cognizant of the trend of the
judicial mind.[5] Most bankers were similarly uninformed.

Meanwhile, a number of states in their efforts to solve the
problem of effectively taxing intangibles had adopted schemes of
classification which imposed on intangibles a much lower rate of
taxation than was imposed on real property.[6] A considerable
number of states also, either by law or custom, exempted mortgages on the ground of double taxation while other states imposed
on such instruments only a small recording fee in lieu of ad
valorem taxation. Several states had adopted an income tax on
the income from intangibles in lieu of a property tax on such
property. In all states having income and classified property
taxes, national bank taxes were now completely voidable. Consequently, there developed a rising tide of bank litigation which
in a few years led to the annulment of all or a part of the share
tax on national banks in a considerable number of states.[7] Nor
did the litigation stop here. State banks began to protest share
taxes under the uniformity clause of state constitutions and the
equal protection clause of the federal constitution. They were
successful in voiding them in a number of cases.[8]

Under such conditions the states affected were faced with the
alternatives of an amendment to the federal law which would
liberalize the permissive tax clause of the National Bank Act, the
complete or partial surrender of their hard-won schemes of classification and income taxation, or compromise bank taxation. Efforts to liberalize the share tax provision of the National Bank

[5] See chap. 3, *infra.*

[6] See S. E. Leland, *The Classified Property Tax* (Boston: Houghton
Mifflin Co., 1928), for a comprehensive treatment of the development of
the classification movement.

[7] See chaps. 4-5, *infra.*

[8] See chaps. 4-5, *infra.*

Act by the 1923 amendment to the federal law were later nullified by the court, but there were added, by the amendments of 1923 and 1926, provisions which permitted the states to tax the net income of banks or to impose an excise tax measured by net income. A further provision authorized the states to tax the dividends from national bank shares as income to the shareholder, either as an alternative or supplement to the income or excise tax. Each of these several methods of bank taxation is subject to specific restrictions which have operated to limit its employment. Wisconsin adopted income taxation of banks, while Massachusetts, New York, Washington,[9] Oregon, California, Alabama, Idaho, Oklahoma, and Utah employ the excise tax. Vermont, alone, taxes the dividend income of banks as an exclusive business tax. For reasons which appear perfectly valid to them the remaining states have retained share taxation. Owing to the invalidity or voidability of share taxes, a number of these states now tax banks as a result of compromise agreements with the bankers. Others have attempted to validate their share taxes by legislative changes in the state code which provide that "other moneyed capital" shall be classified with bank shares, while intangibles not in competition with such shares are taxed at lower rates. Such attempts, however, appear doomed to failure if the position taken in *Public National Bank* v. *Keating*[10] be maintained, since the federal court in that case held that other moneyed capital, as determined by the Supreme Court of New York, was too narrowly defined and that *in fact* there was a huge volume of such competing moneyed capital which was not assessed at the rate applied to bank shares with the result that the bank tax was declared invalid. This decision, affirmed by the highest court in a memorandum deci-

[9] The Washington excise tax on banks was declared unconstitutional. See chap. 6, *infra*.

[10] *Public National Bank* v. *Keating*, 47 F (2d) 561 (1931).

sion,[11] imperils the status of share taxation in those states which attempted thus to circumvent the rulings of the Richmond case. Share taxation of national banks rests, therefore, on extremely tenuous grounds in the thirty-seven states in which it is now in force.

Since 1927 there has been a continuous effort to amend further the federal law to permit the states broader powers in the taxation of national banks. Congressional hearings were conducted in 1928, 1930, 1931, 1933, and 1934 at which representatives of the banks and the states presented their divergent views as to the necessity for an amendment. Efforts of the banks and the tax officials to iron out their differences by negotiation appeared to be successful in 1930 and again in 1932, but the compromise bills agreed upon by the representatives of some of the states failed to meet the approval of the tax officials of other states. Congress in 1934 was apparently deadlocked on the issue, the Senate Committee on Banking and Currency having approved a bill which would continue the protection now afforded national banks and extend it alike to state banks which are members of the Federal Reserve System, while the House Committee favorably reported a measure which would appreciably increase the powers of the states in the taxation of national banks. The issue as yet remains unsolved and share taxation by consent, express or implied, characterizes the situation. Such a condition is extremely unfortunate for the problem of bank taxation transcends the revenues derived from such levies, important as these are to the state and local treasuries. Involved in its solution are the larger issues of classification and income taxation. Until the status of national bank taxation can be more definitely determined, the states cannot safely adopt schemes of classification without openly endangering the legality

[11] *Keating* v. *Public National Bank,* 284 U. S. 578 (1931). See chap. 7, *infra,* for a discussion of this case and another case of somewhat similar import, namely, *Iowa-Des Moines National Bank* v. *Bennett et al,* 284 U. S. 239 (1931).

of their taxes on bank shares. Nor can they adopt the taxation of income from intangibles in lieu of ad valorem taxation without invalidating their share taxes on national banks.

Moreover, the employment of the income or franchise tax methods on national banks, as now authorized by federal law, is so restricted as to compel the states to re-adjust their tax systems in essential respects in order to validate the franchise taxes on national banks. Thus, Congress, in its effort to protect the National Banking System from potentially inimical taxation, has so circumscribed the methods of taxing these institutions that the states are in fact subject to a considerable degree of coercion in the construction of their entire tax structures. In view of these pervasive legal and fiscal complications, the present study attempts, firstly, to trace the evolution of these issues and, secondly, to appraise the several methods of state bank taxation now in force.

CHAPTER II

STATUTORY EVOLUTION OF SECTION 5219,
1864-1923

THE statutory genesis of the state taxation of national banks is to be found in the National Bank Act of 1864. The original act of 1863 contained no provision authorizing the state taxation of national banks, but the debates on the revised measure were enlivened with this issue. Should the banks be subject only to federal taxation or to both federal and state taxation? If the latter, on what constitutional grounds might such taxation rest and by what methods and to what degrees should these banks be taxed by the states?

In both houses of Congress there was a vigorous group which favored the exclusive taxation of national banks by the federal government, but in both bodies the advocates of joint state and federal taxation were victorious.[1] After a number of proposals for state taxation were made in the House, that body passed a tax clause which permitted the states to tax the capital stock, other than that invested in federal bonds, to the same degree that the property of other moneyed corporations was taxed, with the further proviso that the capital, circulation, dividends or business of national banks might be taxed at no higher rate than that imposed by the state on moneyed capital in the hands of individuals.

When the measure reached the Senate, the constitutional phases of the question were elaborately discussed. Senator Sumner of Massachusetts urged that the supremacy of the federal government was of such a character as to free these banks as agencies of that government from the potentially destructive taxes of states, citing the *dictum* of Chief Justice Marshall in *McCulloch v. Maryland*. The advocates of state taxation, while admitting

[1] *Congressional Globe,* 38th Cong., 1st sess., pp. 1412-15, 1682.

that the court had held that the United States Bank and its operations were not subject to state taxation, contended that such immunity did not apply to the shares. Mr. Fessenden of Maine urged that:

. . . this opinion does not deprive the states of any resources which they originally possessed. It does not extend to a tax paid by the real property of the bank, in common with the other real property within the State, nor to a tax imposed on the interest which the citizens of Maryland may hold in this institution, in common with other property of the same description throughout the State.[2]

Senator Collamer drew a distinction between the institution and its shares which were the personal property of the shareholders and taxable as such at the *situs* of the shareholder.[3] Senator Johnson of Maryland, who had heard the case argued before the court, interpreted the decision as declaring that the power of the State of Maryland to tax the shares of the United States Bank was an original power resident in the sovereignty of the state; that while a tax on the franchise or operations of the bank was held invalid by the court,

. . . no judge thought, and no member of the bar who argued the cause dreamed of denying that it would be in the power of the States to tax the property of their citizens invested in the stock of the Bank of the United States . . . and the Supreme Court closed their opinion, so as to exclude any conclusion which could be drawn as against the taxing power of the States on that point by saying that it is to be understood that Maryland has the right, and every State in which there may be a bank of the United States, either the mother bank or a branch, has the right to tax the real estate which the bank may hold within that State, and to tax the shares of her citizens in that institution.[4]

Therefore Senator Johnson concluded that the *federal government lacked the power to exempt from state taxation* the shares of bank stock invested in government bonds.

[2] *Ibid.*, p. 1895.   [3] *Ibid.*, p. 1890.   [4] *Ibid.*, p. 1956.

In the end this view prevailed and the state tax clause of the Senate bill provided for the taxation of the market value of bank shares subject to the restrictions that the rate imposed should not be higher than the rate on other moneyed capital in the hands of individual citizens nor higher than the rate on state bank shares. In the conference committee the Senate provision was adopted with slight changes and the measure became law on June 3, 1864.[5] The state bank clause of the National Bank Act read as follows:

Provided, That nothing in this act shall be construed to prevent all the shares in any of the said associations held by any person or body corporate from being included in the valuation of the personal property of such person or corporation in the assessment of taxes imposed by or under State authority, at the place where such bank is located, and not elsewhere; but not at a greater rate than is assessed upon other moneyed capital in the hands of individual citizens of such State: *Provided further,* That the tax so imposed under the laws of any State upon the shares of any of the associations authorized by this act shall not exceed the rate imposed upon the shares in any of the banks organized under the authority of the State where such association is located, *Provided further,* That nothing in this act shall exempt the real estate of such associations from either State, county or municipal taxes to the same extent, according to its value, as other real estate is taxed.[6]

In order to facilitate the assessment of these shares, as well as safeguard the rights of creditors and shareholders, Section forty of the act provided:

And be it further enacted, That the president and cashier of every such association shall cause to be kept at all times a full and correct list of the names and residences of all the share holders in the association, and the number of shares held by each, in the office where its business is transacted; and such list shall be subject to the inspection of all the shareholders and creditors of the association, *and the officers authorized to assess taxes under State authority,* during business hours of each day in which business may be legally trans-

[5] *Ibid.,* pp. 2622, 2639, 2727.   [6] *Ibid.,* p. 2621.

acted; and a copy of such list, on the first Monday of July in each year, verified by the oath of such president or cashier, shall be transmitted to the comptroller of the currency.[7]

The significance of this provision must not be minimized for it made possible assessment and collection at the source. In so providing, the share tax on banks was destined to become the most effectively enforced of all personal property taxes.

Much has been said in later years as to whether congressional assent was necessary to permit the states to tax national bank shares. The *dicta* of the court in *McCulloch* v. *Maryland* were to the effect that Maryland had original powers residing in its own sovereignty to tax the real estate and the "interest of its citizens" in the United States Bank. The emphasis and respect accorded this decision by the Senate point to the conclusion that it was the intent of that body to make the provision for state taxation of national banks conform to the principle enunciated by Chief Justice Marshall. There was little agitation in the upper house to subject national banks, their capital, or their income to direct taxation, despite the fact that the advocates of some form of state taxation were equally as strong in the Senate as in the House. The obvious intent of the Senate was to confine the taxation of the banks to those types indicated by the court.

To some it has appeared that the fact that Congress saw fit to write into the National Bank Act the provisions relating to state taxation was *ipso facto* the expression of a permissive power delegated by Congress to the states. Otherwise, it was argued, the provision was sheer redundancy. Others hold Section 5219 to be merely a declaratory statute. The answer to this issue is insoluble. The court itself has varied in its interpretation of the character of the statute.[8] Nor was the issue clear in the mind of Congress. Faced with the necessity of protecting from hostile state taxation

[7] *United States Statutes at Large,* XIII, 111. Italics by the writer.
[8] See chap. 3, *infra.*

the federal agency it was in the act of creating, Congress authorized only those types of taxation which the court, in the absence
of express constitutional direction, had indicated were within the
power of the states. In so doing, Congress added legislative sanc-
tion to the principle enunciated by the court. If Congress had
contented itself with a mere declaration that the shares and real
estate were taxable by the states, it would have done nothing more
than to declare in statute what the court had defined, but the fact
that Congress saw fit to place definite limits on such taxation lends
some color to the view that it was, by that action, restricting the
limits of the taxing power of the states with respect to these federal agencies. To that extent, at least, legislative permission
appears to have entered into the statute.

The state tax provision in the National Bank Act of 1864 did
not prove acceptable in one particular to the several states. The
stipulation that the shares should be taxed at the "place where the
bank is located, and not elsewhere" had not in practice met the
administrative needs of some states. Maine, in particular, had
encountered difficulties, the opinion of eminent lawyers of that
state being that national bank shares could not be taxed at all
under the constitution of that state.[9] The fact that personalty,
other than national bank shares, was taxable at the domicile of the
holder rather than at the *situs* of the property raised the issue as
to whether the taxation of bank shares at the *situs* of the bank
was not in violation of the uniformity clause in the state constitution. Massachusetts had resolved this issue by a judicial decision
which broadly interpreted the "place where the bank is located,
and not elsewhere," to mean the state area and not the physical
location of the bank.[10]

To meet these objections an amendment to the law was introduced in 1868 which read:

[9] *Congressional Globe*, 40th Cong., 2d sess., p. 802.
[10] *Austin* v. *Board of Aldermen,* 14 Allen 359 (1867).

That the words "place where the bank is located, and not else-where," in section forty-one of the act to provide a national currency, approved June 3, 1864, shall be construed and held to mean the State within which the bank is located; and the Legislature of each State may determine and direct the manner and place of taxing all the shares of national banks located within said State, subject to the re-striction that the taxation shall not be at a greater rate than is assessed upon other moneyed capital in the hands of individual citizens of such State: *And provided always,* That the shares of any national bank owned by non-residents of any State shall be taxed in the city or town where said bank is located, and not elsewhere.[11]

This bill was immediately passed by the House and the Senate. In the Senate no discussion accompanied its passage, while in the House it was but briefly considered. Mr. Pomeroy stated that there was but a single proposition involved, namely, that the legis-lature of a state shall have the right to tax the shares of residents wherever it sees fit. Curiously enough, Congress, through inad-vertence or in ignorance of the provisions of the amendment, over-looked the fact that one test of the rate of taxation to be levied on national bank shares was dropped. The Act of 1864 had re-stricted the rate to that (1) on other moneyed capital and (2) on state banks. The amendment of 1868 retained only the moneyed capital limit.

Much has been said in recent years as to the intent of Con-gress in regard to the limiting restrictions on the rate of taxation on national bank shares. One authority states:

There is no finally conclusive evidence as to what was meant by the expression "other moneyed capital in the hands of individual citizens;" but to the writer the evidence is persuasive in favor of the construction that the reference was to the stock of state banks, and not to personal investments. There were no other important com-peting banking and financial institutions at that time, and the whole discussion indicates that Congress desired to preserve equality of

[11] *Congressional Globe,* 40th Cong., 2d sess., p. 802.

taxation between the national banks and their natural competitors in the banking business.[12]

The issue of congressional intent is unquestionably clouded in doubt. Congress probably did not envisage the issues which were to arise from classification and income taxation. But there appears to be a strong possibility that Congress had in mind, as the restricting limit on the taxation of national bank shares, the rate on personal property in the form of other moneyed capital. The necessity for some limit arose out of the contention of those favoring exclusive federal taxation that the states would tax these federal agencies out of existence. The advocates of state taxation in the House countered this argument by citing the uniformity clause in state constitutions and by further proposing specific limits on bank taxation, such as the rate on other corporations and the rate on the property of other moneyed corporations. In the Senate when the issue of taxation was narrowed more particularly to the taxation of national bank shares as a part of the personal estate of the shareholder the generally expressed limit on such taxation was the rate on other moneyed capital.

The second limit to the rate in the Act of 1864 was largely in the nature of an afterthought which received but little attention at the time of its passage. It was dropped in 1868 without a murmur of protest from anyone interested in maintaining equality of national and state bank taxes. Of some significance is the observation of Senator Fessenden, when this second proviso was proposed, that it was already covered by the preceding restriction. And when the bill, as agreed upon by the conference committee, was presented to the House for action, Mr. Noble of Ohio asked: "I wish to know how the bill stands in reference to the right of States to tax these banks for state purposes."[13] To which Mr. Hooper of the conference committee replied, "It leaves the right

[12] H. L. Lutz, "Evolution of Section 5219," *Bul.* N. T. A., XIII, 211.
[13] *Congressional Globe,* 38th Cong., 1st sess., p. 2639.

to the States to tax these banks at the same rate as they tax other moneyed capital in the State."[14]

There is much to lead one to the conclusion that Congress, in providing for the taxation of national bank shares as a part of the personal estate of the holder, had in mind as the primary limitation thereon the rate on other moneyed capital, which concept was not identical to that of state bank shares. Competing moneyed capital was not at that time restricted to state banks. Innumerable private lenders and unincorporated private bankers were then doing a substantial business. There had been keen opposition to the incorporated bank in several states. Iowa had prohibited banks for several years[15] and Wisconsin required a popular referendum on the issue of a general banking law which was not passed until 1852.[16] Texas, while not a part of the Union in 1864, prohibited incorporated state banks until 1869. In that state, in 1859, 3,053 money lenders were assessed to the amount of $3,330,038.[17] The words "other moneyed capital" were not, therefore, meaningless symbols which could not be differentiated from bank shares at the time the act was passed. The anti-bank movement, while past flood tide, still had its votaries.[18]

An interesting contemporary legal opinion on the amended law is refreshing in view of the discussion which has centered in recent years around this provision. An attorney, Mr. B. F. Thomas, upon the request for an interpretation of the new law by the Boston Clearing House said:

[14] *Ibid.*

[15] J. H. Brindley, *History of Taxation in Iowa* (Iowa City, 1911), p. 146.

[16] R. V. Phelan, *The Financial History of Wisconsin* (Bulletin of the University of Wisconsin, No. 193, 1908), p. 414.

[17] E. T. Miller, *A Financial History of Texas* (Bulletin of the University of Texas, No. 37, 1916), pp. 107, 159.

[18] L. C. Helderman, *National and State Banks: A Study of Their Origins* (Boston: Houghton Mifflin Co., 1931), chap. 5.

If Congress was looking to the contingency that different rates might be fixed by the State upon different kinds of moneyed capital, my strong impression would be that the tax laid by the State upon the bank shares could not exceed the lowest of such rates; that Congress did not intend to subject the shares of the banks to the highest rate of taxation any State might see fit to fix upon any form of moneyed capital in the State. Such tax might be laid for the purpose of advancing the tax upon the stock of the national bank.[19]

By dropping, in 1868, the second limitation on the tax rate on national bank shares, Congress paved the way for a long drawn out controversy on the meaning of the first limitation, and an emphatic demand for a clarifying and liberalizing amendment.

In summary, the provisions of the act, as amended in 1868, stipulated that the states could tax the real estate of national banks to the banks to the same extent that other real estate was taxed, and the shares of national banks could be taxed to the shareholder, subject only to two restrictions: first, that the shares of non-residents should be taxed at the *situs* of the bank; and, second, that the rate on the shares could not be greater than that on "other moneyed capital in the hands of individuals."

The amendment of 1868 to the state tax provision of the National Bank Act of 1864 was the only statutory change made in this provision until 1923, with the exception of slight changes in the phraseology incident to the general revision of federal statutes in 1878. By this revision the provision became Section 5219 of the United States Revised Statutes and read as follows: (Italics denote change)

Nothing *herein* shall prevent all the shares in any association from being included in the valuation of the personal property of *the owner or holder of such shares,* in *assessing* taxes imposed by authority *of the State within which* the association is located: *but the legislature of each State may determine and direct the manner and place of taxing*

[19] B. F. Thomas, "The Taxation of National Bank Shares," *Bankers Magazine,* XXIII (1869), 454.

all the shares of national banking associations located within the State, subject only to the two restrictions, that the taxation shall not be at a greater rate than is assessed upon other moneyed capital in the hands of individual citizens of such State, and that the shares of any national banking *association* owned by non-residents of any State shall be taxed in the city or town where the bank is located, and not elsewhere. Nothing *herein shall be construed* to exempt the real *property* of associations from either State, county, or municipal taxes, to the same extent, according to its value, as other real *property* is taxed.

CHAPTER III

THE INTERPRETATION OF SECTION 5219 BY THE UNITED STATES SUPREME COURT

THE perusal of the few lines which comprise Section 5219 does not reveal clearly the scope of this law. A careful survey of the numerous relevant decisions of the Supreme Court of the United States alone demonstrates its ramifications.

Certain powers the states[1] clearly do not have. The states cannot tax any property of the bank other than its real property,[2] save only the investment in shares of other national banks. Nor could a license or franchise tax be levied against a national bank until the amendment of 1926 so provided.[3] Exemption of the assets of the banks, other than the real property, extends likewise to insolvent banks in the hands of receivers,[4] but the shares of such insolvent banks, if of any value, are taxable. While the shares are taxable, the capital may not be assessed.[5] Assessment of shares *in solido* is not permissible if operating as a tax on the bank.[6] Finally, states cannot tax the shares of state banks owned by national banks, but they may tax the shares of national banks

[1] Defined to include territories. *Talbott* v. *Silver Bow County*, 139 U. S. 438 (1891).

[2] *Bradley* v. *The People*, 4 Wall 459 (1866); *Rosenblatt* v. *Johnston*, 104 U. S. 462 (1881); *Owensboro National Bank* v. *Owensboro*, 173 U. S. 664 (1899); *Third National Bank of Louisville* v. *Stone*, 174 U. S. 432 (1899); *Home Savings Bank* v. *Des Moines*, 205 U. S. 503 (1907); *Bank of California* v. *Richardson*, 248 U. S. 476 (1919); *First National Bank of Gulfport* v. *Adams*, 258 U. S. 362 (1922).

[3] *Owensboro National Bank* v. *Owensboro*, 173 U. S. 664 (1899). See chap. 6, *infra*, for franchise tax as authorized in 1926.

[4] *Rosenblatt* v. *Johnston*, 104 U. S. 462 (1881).

[5] *National Bank* v. *Commonwealth*, 9 Wall 353 (1869); *Aberdeen Bank* v. *Chehalis County*, 166 U. S. 440 (1897); *Third National Bank of St. Louis* v. *Stone*, 174 U. S. 432 (1899).

[6] *Aberdeen Bank* v. *Chehalis County*, 166 U. S. 440 (1897).

owned by another national bank.[7]   However, the taxable value of
such national bank shares, so held, may be deducted from the
value of the bank's own shares.[8]   The theory underlying these
limitations on the state taxing power is that the federal government in its own sphere possesses sovereign powers and its agencies,
in this instance national banks, are immune from the potentially
destructive taxation of the states.[9]

The positive taxing powers of the states with respect to national banks also are limited.   Both by statutory enactment and
by judicial interpretation the real estate owned by national banks
is taxable to the bank in the same degree that other real estate is
taxed.[10]   Whether or not "real property" in Section 5219 includes
the furniture and fixtures of a bank has not as yet been adjudi-
cated by the United States Supreme Court.   Since the term "real
property" was substituted for "real estate" in the revision of
federal laws in 1878, it is reasonable to assume that no change in
meaning was contemplated.   Both the practice of assessing officers
and the decisions of state courts vary on this issue.

In addition to the real property of national banks, national
bank shares are taxable to the stockholder.   In determining the
basis for the taxation of such shares, the court, from the begin-
ning, took the position anticipated by Senator Johnson and others
in the debate on the bill;[11] namely, that the interest of the stockholder and that of the corporation are separate and distinct properties.   Therefore, a tax on the shares is not a tax on the capital
of the bank.[12]   Consequently, the stockholder may be taxed on
the full value, and not merely a fractional part, of his interest

[7] *Bank of Redemption* v. *Boston*, 125 U. S. 60 (1888) ; *Bank of California* v. *Richardson*, 248 U. S. 476 (1919).
[8] *Bank of California* v. *Richardson*, 248 U. S. 476 (1919).
[9] *McCulloch* v. *State of Maryland*, 4 Wheaton 316 (1819).
[10] *Owensboro National Bank* v. *Owensboro*, 173 U. S. 664 (1899).
[11] See chap. 2, *supra*.
[12] *Van Allen* v. *The Assessors*, 3 Wall 573 (1865).

therein. The court has consistently followed[13] its rulings in this respect with but one exception.[14]

The practical significance of this principle is far reaching. The occasion for the enunciation of the rule arose out of the efforts of banks to deduct from the value of the shares the amount of their holdings of tax exempt government securities, their argument being that to tax the full value of the shares was in effect the forbidden taxation[15] of the securities themselves. The court denied the validity of this contention in the Van Allen case. In view of the large holdings of government securities by national banks the permission of such deductions would nullify all share taxes.[16] For similar reasons, the Federal Reserve Bank stock owned by national banks may not be deducted from the shares of national banks.[17] But, as previously indicated, the taxable value of shares of national bank stock held by another national bank is deductible.[18]

The principle of the taxation of the full value of the stockholder's interest early led the court to the conclusion that the

[13] *People* v. *Commissioners*, 4 Wall 244 (1866); *National Bank* v. *Commonwealth*, 9 Wall 353 (1869); *Evansville Bank* v. *Britton*, 105 U. S. 322 (1881); *Bank of Commerce* v. *Tennessee*, 161 U. S. 134 (1896); *New Orleans* v. *Citizens Bank*, 167 U. S. 371 (1897); *Owensboro National Bank* v. *Owensboro*, 173 U. S. 664 (1899); *Cleveland Trust Company* v. *Lander*, 184 U. S. 111 (1902); *Home Savings Bank* v. *Des Moines*, 205 U. S. 503 (1907); *Peoples National Bank of Kingfisher* v. *Board of Equalization*, 260 U. S. 702 (1922); *Des Moines National Bank* v. *Fairweather*, 263 U. S. 103 (1923).

[14] *Bank of California* v. *Richardson*, 248 U. S. 476 (1919). Within five years the court reaffirmed and has since maintained its original position. See *Des Moines National Bank* v. *Fairweather*, 263 U. S. 103 (1923).

[15] *Weston* v. *City Council of Charleston*, 2 Peters 449 (1829); *The Banks* v. *The Mayor*, 7 Wall 16 (1868); *Banks* v. *Supervisors*, 7 Wall 26 (1868).

[16] The book value of national bank shares on June 30, 1931, was $3,625,131,000 and these banks held $4,253,488,000 of exempt government securities.

[17] *Des Moines National Bank* v. *Fairweather*, 263 U. S. 103 (1923).

[18] *Bank of California* v. *Richardson*, 248 U. S. 476 (1919).

shares were taxable above par value.[19] This principle further implies that the states are not required by the federal statute to allow a bank to deduct the value of its real property from the value of its shares, though such is the common practice.[20] Irrespective of the property in which the share capital is invested, the full value of the shares is subject to taxation if the states so require.

How may the state reach such shares? Intangibles have a way of disappearing on the day of assessment.[21] Protection against such evasion by national bank stockholders is assured through assessment and collection at the source. Section forty of the National Bank Act provided that every bank shall keep a stockholders' list which shall be open to the assessing officers during business hours. Assessment at the source being made possible by statutory provision, judicial interpretation sanctioned collection at the source.[22] Accordingly, the bank may be used as an agent of the stockholder to collect the tax and may reimburse itself from the dividends or other income to be distributed to the shareholder, and may bring suit in behalf of the stockholder.[23] These superior administrative features insured the effective taxation of national bank shares in practically all the states in marked contrast to the evasion of a large proportion of other intangibles when subjected to the general property levy.[24]

[19] *Hepburn* v. *The School Directors,* 23 Wall 480 (1874); *People* v. *The Commissioners,* 94 U. S. 415 (1876).

[20] *Commercial Bank* v. *Chambers,* 182 U. S. 556 (1901); *Amoskeag Savings Bank* v. *Purdy,* 231 U. S. 373 (1913).

[21] Leland, *op. cit.,* pp. 27-30, 131.

[22] *National Bank* v. *Commonwealth,* 9 Wall 353 (1869); *Lionberger* v. *Rouse,* 9 Wall 468 (1869); *Tappan* v. *Merchants' National Bank,* 19 Wall 490 (1873); *Waite* v. *Dowley,* 94 U. S. 527 (1876); *Citizens National Bank* v. *Commonwealth of Kentucky,* 217 U. S. 443 (1910).

[23] *Cummings* v. *National Bank,* 101 U. S. 153 (1879); *Hills* v. *Exchange Bank,* 105 U. S. 319 (1881); *Citizens National Bank* v. *Commonwealth,* 217 U. S. 443 (1910).

[24] Leland, *op. cit.,* pp. 411 ff.

Another question of administrative procedure is that of tax *situs*. Section 5219 prescribes that the national bank shares held by non-residents shall be taxed at the *situs* of the bank. The fact that the shares of a national bank are held by a national bank situated in another state does not preclude their taxation by the state in which the bank is situated.[25] While the rule of business *situs* applies to the shares held by non-residents, the state may assess the shares of residents at their domicile or at the location of the bank.[26]

Though the states were restricted until 1923 to the taxation of the real property and the shares, they could impose a tax on the savings deposits in a national bank to the depositor, and the bank, if it so agrees, could pay the tax thereon.[27] While in legal contemplation such a tax is a levy on the depositor, it often falls on the bank. The successful use of this method[28] of indirect taxation of banks by certain states in New England gives rise to some wonder that other states have not resorted to similar impositions. Ohio and Indiana adopted this device in 1931 and 1933, respectively.[29]

The specific limitations on the state taxation of national bank shares is really the heart of the present problem. The original act of 1864 provided two limitations, (1) the rate on other moneyed capital and (2) the tax burden on state banks. The Amendment of 1868 dropped the latter limit and left the shares of national banks to be taxed as the legislature of each state might determine, save only (1) that non-resident shares must be taxed at the *situs* of the bank, if taxed at all, and (2) "that the taxation shall not be at a greater rate than is assessed upon other moneyed capital in the hands of individual citizens of such State."

[25] *Bank of Redemption* v. *Boston,* 125 U. S. 60 (1888).
[26] *Tappan* v. *Merchants National Bank,* 19 Wall 490 (1873).
[27] *Clement National Bank* v. *State of Vermont,* 231 U. S. 120 (1913).
[28] Leland, *op. cit.,* pp. 218 ff.
[29] *Laws of Ohio,* 1931, p. 722 as amended by *Laws of Ohio,* 1933, S. B. No. 30; *Acts,* Indiana, 1933, chap. 83.

The purpose of Congress in providing these limits on the state taxation of national banks was, in the opinion of the court, to prevent the states from favoring competitors of national banks and thus discriminating against them.[30] With respect to the "rate of taxation" the court has held that the phrase refers to the rate on *taxable* moneyed capital;[31] hence the exemption of certain properties,[32] such as that of schools, churches, and charitable institutions and municipal bonds,[33] does not affect the rate on national bank shares.

The rate of taxation, moreover, includes the entire process of valuation and assessment.[34] Discriminations may arise as a result of different rules of valuation quite as effectively as by using different percentages in computing the taxes on fixed valuations. Since the restriction in Section 5219 does not require that the state shall apply the same mode of taxation to national bank shares that it applies to other property provided no injustice, inequality, or unfriendly discrimination arises therefrom,[35] the rate of taxation must refer to "the actual incidence and practical burden of the tax upon the tax payer."[36] Little effort has been made to inquire into the incidence of taxation either on banks or competing moneyed capital in the cases presented to the court. For

[30] *Lionberger* v. *Rouse*, 9 Wall 468 (1869); *Adams* v. *Nashville*, 95 U. S. 19 (1877); *Boyer* v. *Boyer*, 113 U. S. 689 (1885); *Mercantile Bank* v. *New York*, 121 U. S. 138 (1887); *First National Bank of Garnett* v. *Ayers*, 160 U. S. 660 (1896); *First National Bank of Wellington* v. *Chapman*, 173 U. S. 205 (1899); *Amoskeag Bank* v. *Purdy*, 231 U. S. 373 (1913); *Bank of California* v. *Richardson*, 248 U. S. 476 (1919); *Des Moines* v. *Fairweather*, 263 U. S. 103 (1923); *First National Bank of Guthrie Center* v. *Anderson,* 269 U. S. 341 (1926).

[31] *People* v. *The Commissioner*, 4 Wall 244 (1866).

[32] *Adams* v. *Nashville*, 95 U. S. 19 (1877).

[33] *Boyer* v. *Boyer*, 113 U. S. 689 (1885); *Des Moines National Bank* v. *Fairweather*, 263 U. S. 103 (1923).

[34] *People* v. *Weaver*, 100 U. S. 539 (1879).

[35] *Covington* v. *First National Bank of Covington*, 198 U. S. 100 (1905); *Amoskeag Savings Bank* v. *Purdy*, 231 U. S. 373 (1913).

[36] *Amoskeag Savings Bank* v. *Purdy*, 231 U. S. 373, 386 (1913).

the most part it has been merely an issue of impact. The court has been concerned only with the *effective* rate on these shares.

What inequalities constitute discrimination? Exact mathematical equality of burden is not required.[37] Some differences in the rates of taxation are not discriminatory within the meaning of the restriction. The fact that two state banks operating in Missouri were exempted, by virtue of charter rights, from all taxation save only 1 per cent on their paid-in capital, while national bank shares were subject to a rate of 2 per cent did not constitute a discrimination, as the state of Missouri had complied to the extent of its ability with the requirements of the federal statute.[38] Again, the assessment of bank shares at market while bonds and mortgages were assessed at par or nominal value did not constitute a discrimination.[39] The fact that national banks may not deduct from the value of their shares the amount of their capital invested in real property situated outside the state does not produce a discrimination against the bank,[40] though the court later suggested that it might be argued that such a deduction was within the intent of Section 5219.[41] Nor does the deduction of the debts of unincorporated bankers from their credits constitute a discrimination against national banks;[42] and, similarly, the deduction of tax exempt bonds from the assets of private bankers is not violative of the rule of substantial equality.[43] The state can exempt moneyed

[37] *Lionberger* v. *Rouse*, 9 Wall 468 (1869); *Tappan* v. *Merchants' National Bank*, 19 Wall 490 (1873); *National Bank* v. *Kimball*, 103 U. S. 732 (1880); *Boyer* v. *Boyer*, 113 U. S. 689 (1885); *Davenport Bank* v. *Davenport*, 123 U. S. 83 (1887); *First National Bank of Wellington* v. *Chapman*, 173 U. S. 205 (1899); *First National Bank of Guthrie Center* v. *Anderson*, 269 U. S. 341 (1926).

[38] *Lionberger* v. *Rouse*, 9 Wall 468 (1869).

[39] *Hepburn* v. *The School Directors*, 23 Wall 480 (1874).

[40] *Commercial Bank* v. *Chambers*, 182 U. S. 556 (1901).

[41] *First National Bank* v. *Albright*, 208 U. S. 548 (1908).

[42] *First National Bank of Wellington* v. *Chapman*, 173 U. S. 205 (1899).

[43] *Des Moines National Bank* v. *Fairweather*, 263 U. S. 103 (1923).

capital, such as deposits in savings banks or funds of charitable institutions, if such exemption is for reasons of public policy without producing thereby a discrimination against national bank shares.[44]

In regard to the competitive status of savings banks, the court has varied in its position. In the three earlier cases[45] involving such banks the position assumed was that deposits of savings banks were not in real competition with national banks. In *Aberdeen* v. *Chehalis County,* they were recognized as belonging to the *genus* of competing moneyed capital, but the fact that the exemption from taxation was for reasons of public policy, and not as an unfriendly discrimination against national banks, prevented such exemption from invalidating the taxes on national bank shares.[46]

The rule of equality of treatment, it is to be noted, applies as between national bank stockholders and holders of other moneyed capital. Discrimination as between shareholders of the same national bank, or as between stockholders of different national banks are not prohibited by the court.[47] The fact that the shares owned by non-residents may be taxed only at the *situs* of the national bank, while the shares owned by residents may be taxed either there or at the domicile of the owner makes equality of tax burden as between shareholders of the same institution contingent upon the administrative policies of the states.

[44] *Aberdeen Bank* v. *Chehalis County,* 166 U. S. 440 (1897); *Mercantile Bank* v. *New York,* 121 U. S. 138 (1887); *Davenport Bank* v. *Davenport Board of Equalization,* 123 U. S. 83 (1887); *Bank of Redemption* v. *Boston,* 125 U. S. 60 (1888).

[45] *Mercantile Bank* v. *New York,* 121 U. S. 138 (1887); *Davenport Bank* v. *Davenport Board of Equalization,* 123 U. S. 83 (1887); *Bank of Redemption* v. *Boston,* 125 U. S. 60 (1888).

[46] *Aberdeen* v. *Chehalis County,* 166 U. S. 440 (1897).

[47] *Merchants' and Manufacturers' Bank* v. *Pennsylvania,* 167 U. S. 461 (1897); *Covington* v. *Covington First National Bank,* 185 U. S. 270 (1902); *Citizens National Bank* v. *Commonwealth of Kentucky,* 217 U. S. 443 (1910); *Amoskeag Savings Bank* v. *Purdy,* 231 U. S. 373 (1913).

One other type of innocuous inequality should be noted.   In *Hepburn* v. *The School Directors* the court held that a *partial exemption* of other moneyed capital did not constitute a discrimination against national bank shares.   In that case all mortgages, judgments, recognizances, and moneys owing upon articles of agreement for the sale of real estate were exempt from the taxation.   In spite of these facts the court held that there might be some moneyed capital in the community which was taxed, and hence no discrimination existed against national banks.[48]

In a number of cases the court has found actual discriminations.   Before these discriminations can be intelligently analyzed it is essential first to examine the interpretations of the courts as to what constitutes "other moneyed capital in the hands of individual citizens."   Several considerations compel a careful canvass of the court's interpretation of this phrase.   The charges of gross judicial inconsistency have been so general as to cause the court to take notice thereof and to affirm its own consistency.[49]   Again, it has been urged that the phrase has no meaning in either law or economics.   "It is a sack, a catch-all phrase which will hold as much or as little as the courts choose to empty into it."[50]   Finally, the multitude of suits in state and federal courts involving discriminations of this type emphasize the necessity of finding out, if possible, what the court conceives such property to be.

The court in defining the limits of the disputed phrase has resorted to the usual methods of exclusion and inclusion.   Certain investments, the value of which is expressed in terms of money, are outside the category of moneyed capital.   For reasons of public policy, as already indicated, bonds issued under state authority and deposits in savings banks are excluded from the list of other moneyed capital.   Nor was the stock of insurance companies in-

[48] *Hepburn* v. *The School Directors*, 23 Wall 480 (1874).

[49] *First National Bank of Guthrie Center* v. *Anderson*, 269 U. S. 341 (1926).

[50] Lutz, "Evolution of Section 5219," *Bul.* N. T. A. XIII, 212.

cluded within its scope.[51] Likewise, railroad shares, investments in manufacturing and mining companies or "any other corporation of that description" are excluded.[52] Investments in telephone companies, as well as wharf[53] and gas companies,[54] are not competitive with national banks, and their exemption does not invalidate the tax on national bank shares.

Though the court experienced little difficulty in ruling these investments outside moneyed capital, it found itself in great straits when the issue of investments in trust companies was presented for adjudication. In the first consideration of this issue the court, after recounting the powers conferred on trust companies by the New York law, expressed the view that such institutions were not banks, and then further alleged that the evidence presented did not prove the rate on trust companies to be in fact lower than that imposed on banks.[55]

The issue was raised again in *Jenkins* v. *Neff*. Here it was contended that the conditions were different from those obtaining in *Mercantile Bank* v. *New York* since an amendment to the New York law had increased the powers of trust companies to such an extent as to bring them into competition with national banks. But the court, though admitting that the trust companies come into "limited competition" with national banks, did not find any intention on the part of the state to discriminate against national banks.[56] In a later case, however, the court recognized trust com-

[51] *People* v. *The Commissioners*, 4 Wall 244 (1866) ; *Mercantile Bank* v. *New York*, 121 U. S. 138 (1887) ; *Bank of Redemption* v. *Boston*, 125 U. S. 60 (1888) ; *Aberdeen Bank* v. *Chehalis County*, 166 U. S. 440 (1897).

[52] *Mercantile Bank* v. *New York*, 121 U. S. 138 (1887) ; *Talbot* v. *Silver Bow County*, 139 U. S. 438 (1891).

[53] *Bank of Redemption* v. *Boston*, 125 U. S. 60 (1888).

[54] *Aberdeen Bank* v. *Chehalis County*, 166 U. S. 440 (1897).

[55] *Mercantile Bank* v. *New York*, 121 U. S. 138 (1887).

[56] *Jenkins* v. *Neff*, 186 U. S. 230 (1902).

pany shares as competitive moneyed capital.[57]   But the issue of discrimination was not raised in that instance.   Thus, the status of investments in trust companies in relation to Section 5219 is not certain.   It is difficult to see how the courts fairly can exclude them from this category since national banks have been given power to engage in extensive trust operations,[58] and these expanded powers would apparently broaden, as in the analogous case of real estate mortgages,[59] the limits of other moneyed capital.

The first case which called forth a positive definition of other moneyed capital was *Hepburn* v. *The School Directors,* in which the court said:

> We cannot concede that money at interest is the only moneyed capital included in that term as here used by Congress. The words are "other moneyed capital." That certainly makes stock in these banks moneyed capital, and securities might be included in that descriptive term.[60]

This broad definition would include, inferentially, practically all securities since both stock and bonds were enumerated by the court.   Seven years later further content was given to the concept when the court held that credits, rights, demands, and money at interest, as used in the Indiana statute, were moneyed capital.[61] In this case the court distinguished moneyed capital from the category of personal property.

In 1885 the court was forced to adjudicate a second case from Pennsylvania in which railroad securities, shares of certain corporations, mortgages, judgments, recognizances, corporate bonds, and moneys due on contracts for the sale of real estate were exempted from local taxes.   The amounts of involved properties

[57] *Amoskeag* v. *Purdy,* 231 U. S. 373 (1913).

[58] *United States Statutes at Large,* XLIV, 1224-30.

[59] *First National Bank of Guthrie Center* v. *Anderson,* 269 U. S. 341 (1926).

[60] *Hepburn* v. *The School Directors,* 23 Wall 480, 484 (1874).

[61] *Evansville Bank* v. *Britton,* 105 U. S. 322 (1881).

were admittedly large, and state banks were subject to the same local tax as was imposed on national bank shares. The court concluded that the amount of other moneyed capital so exempt was substantial and gave the sought-for relief.[62] Relative to the claim of the counsel that equality of taxation as between state and national bank shares was all that the federal statute required, the court observed:

If by this language it is meant that an illegal discrimination against capital invested in national bank shares cannot exist where no higher rate or heavier burden of taxation is imposed upon them than upon capital invested in state bank shares, or in state savings institutions, we have to say that such is not a proper construction of the act of Congress. *Capital invested in national bank shares was intended to be placed upon the same footing of substantial equality in respect of taxation by State authority, as the State establishes for other moneyed capital in the hands of individual citizens, however invested, whether in State bank shares or otherwise.*[63]

The court in this case took cognizance of the effect of the Amendment of 1868 to Section 5219 as requiring equality of treatment not only as between national banks and state banks, but also between national banks and moneyed capital not invested in state bank shares.

The success of the attorneys for the bank in *Boyer* v. *Boyer* led them to other fields of conquest. They turned to New York City where the bankers, taking comfort from this decision, appointed a committee to consider the advisability of a suit to prevent the collection of bank taxes.[64] This committee reported that, in view of the fact that there was estimated moneyed capital in the hands of individual citizens in the state of New York to the amount of at least $1,778 millions of which not more than $262 millions was taxed, the banks of New York would have a better

[62] *Boyer* v. *Boyer,* 113 U. S. 689 (1885).

[63] *Ibid.,* p. 702. Italics by the writer.

[64] *Bankers Magazine,* XL, 68.

case than in *Boyer* v. *Boyer*. It consequently recommended that joint suit be undertaken, and that the counsel employed in *Boyer* v. *Boyer* be engaged upon a retainer fee of $100 from each bank and a contingent fee not to exceed 10 per cent of the one year's saving in tax.[65]

The result was the presentation of the issues in *Mercantile Bank* v. *New York*. Since the court, in its previous definition of other moneyed capital, had emphasized the amount of such privileged moneyed capital, the strategy of the counsel for the banks was to storm the judicial fortress with quantitative data. It was alleged that under the New York laws there was the material exemption of other moneyed capital of the following species and amounts: corporate shares, other than those of banks, trust and insurance companies, totalling $755,018,892; trust and insurance company shares of $32,018,900; and shares of life insurance companies of $3,540,000, which companies in turn owned mortgages, bonds, and stock of $195,257,305; savings banks and deposits therein of $437,107,501, with an accumulated surplus of $68,669,000; certain municipal bonds of New York City totalling $13,467,000; and shares of stocks of foreign corporations in the hands of their holders equalling $250,000,000.[66] Obviously, if the court was to rely solely on the quantity test, the facts seem to favor the banks.

But the court found no discrimination existed against national bank shares and, in so doing, evolved a further definition of other moneyed capital. Since the purpose of Congress was to prevent unequal and unfriendly competition with national banks by favoritism shown competing moneyed capital, "The *true test of the distinction . . . can only be found in the nature of the business in which the corporation is engaged.*"[67] And what is the business of banking? To this the court replied,

[65] *Ibid.*
[66] *Mercantile Bank* v. *New York*, 121 U. S. 138 (1887).
[67] *Ibid.*, p. 154. Italics by the writer.

The business of banking as defined by law and custom, consists in the issue of notes payable on demand; intended to circulate as money where the banks are banks of issue; in receiving deposits payable on demand; in discounting commercial paper; making loans of money on collateral security; buying and selling bills of exchange; negotiating loans, and dealing in negotiable securities issued by the government, state and national, and municipal and other corporations. These are the operations in which the capital invested in national banks is employed, and it is the nature of that employment which constitutes it in the eye of this statute "moneyed capital." Corporations and individuals carrying on these operations do come into competition with the business of national banks, and capital in the hands of individuals thus employed is what is intended to be described by the act of Congress.[68]

So it is not the form of the investment nor the fact that a corporation may have a large part of its capital invested in securities, payable in money, which distinguishes such funds as "other moneyed capital." It is, rather, the nature of the business and the character of its operations which determine its status. Hence shares of railroad, mining, insurance, and other like corporations are outside the scope of the category, for such companies are not engaged in the business of banking, nor do they participate in the operations which banks perform. As to what is included in the concept the court said,

The terms of the act of Congress . . . include shares of stock or other interests owned by individuals in all enterprises in which the capital employed in carrying on its business is money, where the object of the business is the making of profit by its use as money. The moneyed capital thus employed is invested for that purpose in securities by way of loan, discount, or otherwise, which are from time to time, according to the rules of the business reduced again to money and reinvested. It includes money in the hands of individuals employed in similar way, invested in loans, or in securities for the payment of money, either as an investment of a permanent character, or temporarily with a view to sale or repayment and reinvestment. In

[68] *Ibid.*, p. 156.

this way moneyed capital in the hands of individuals is distinguished from what is known generally as personal property.[69]

In this epochal decision the first vital distinction between moneyed capital and investments valued in terms of money is drawn. It is the competitive employment of funds by individuals and corporations in those operations and transactions characteristic of the business of banking. Such moneys, so used in discounts, loans, and investments of the types in which national banks engage, are moneyed capital in the hands of individual citizens. In ruling that only *competitive* moneyed capital was within the meaning of Section 5219 the court made new law.[70] The definition evolved in this decision has been repeatedly affirmed.[71]

Moneyed capital was again sharply defined in 1921 in *Merchants' National Bank of Richmond* v. *City of Richmond*. This case involved the validity of a state law taxing bank shares at 35 cents per $100 and a city ordinance imposing a tax on them of $1.40 per $100, while bonds, notes and other evidences of indebtedness were taxed at a combined rate of 95 cents per $100. The counsel for the City of Richmond rested his case on the ill-founded contention that Section 5219 required only equality of tax treat-

[69] *Ibid.*, p. 157.

[70] T. R. Powell, "Indirect Encroachment on Federal Authority by the Taxing Powers of the States," *Harvard Law Review*, XXXI, 353.

[71] *Davenport Bank* v. *Davenport Board of Equalization*, 123 U. S. 83 (1887); *Palmer* v. *McMahon*, 133 U. S. 661 (1890); *Talbott* v. *Silver Bow County*, 139 U. S. 438 (1891); *First National Bank of Garnett* v. *Ayers*, 160 U. S. 660 (1896); *Aberdeen Bank* v. *Chehalis County*, 166 U. S. 440 (1897); *First National Bank of Wellington* v. *Chapman*, 173 U. S. 205 (1899); *Jenkins* v. *Neff*, 186 U. S. 230 (1902); *Amoskeag Savings Bank* v. *Purdy*, 231 U. S. 373 (1913); *Merchants' National Bank of Richmond* v. *Richmond*, 256 U. S. 635 (1921); *Des Moines Bank* v. *Fairweather*, 263 U. S. 103 (1923); *First National Bank of Guthrie Center* v. *Anderson*, 269 U. S. 341 (1926); *First National Bank of Hartford, Wisconsin*, v. *City of Hartford*, 273 U. S. 548 (1927); *Minnesota* v. *First National Bank of St. Paul*, 273 U. S. 561 (1927); *Georgetown National Bank* v. *McFarland*, 273 U. S. 567 (1927); *Montana National Bank of Billings* v. *Yellowstone County*, 276 U. S. 499 (1928).

ment as between national and state banks. But the court called attention to its interpretation of the effect of the Amendment of 1868 as stated in *Boyer* v. *Boyer,* and redefined moneyed capital as including:

... not only moneys invested in private banking, properly so-called, but investments of individuals in securities that represent money at interest and other evidences of indebtedness such as normally enter into the business of banking.[72]

This decision raised protests and charges of inconsistency, but no change in position is apparent in this highly dramatized case.[73]

In a later case[74] the court enumerated explicitly real estate mortgages as competitive moneyed capital, the court taking judicial notice of the amendment to the National Bank Act which authorized national banks to lend on real estate mortgages. However, in a more recent decision in which a tendency to narrow the basis for bank tax invalidities was in evidence, the court was not convinced that the mere ownership of real estate mortgages by national banks proved that they loaned money on real estate as such mortgages may have been taken to secure other loans.[75]

The significance of the court's interpretation of other moneyed capital can best be gathered from an examination of the cases in which discriminations against national bank shares were found to exist. Most of these discriminations involve the moneyed capital limit on state taxation. However, some involve only discrimination as between state and national banks. Thus a tax

[72] *Merchants' National Bank of Richmond* v. *City of Richmond,* 256 U. S. 635, 639 (1921).

[73] For the political significance and results of the decision see chaps. 4-5, *infra.*

[74] *First National Bank of Guthrie Center* v. *Anderson,* 269 U. S. 341 (1926). Compare with *Aberdeen* v. *Chehalis County,* 166 U. S. 440 (1897) in which the court had enumerated "investments in mortgages" as being excluded from other moneyed capital.

[75] *First National Bank of Shreveport* v. *Louisiana Tax Commission,* 289 U. S. 60 (1933).

on the capital of state banks, which permits a deduction of the tax exempt securities held by them, while national bank shares are fully taxed to the holder, constitutes a discrimination against such shares and invalidates the tax thereon.[76] As previously observed, the deduction of the tax exempt bonds of an unincorporated private banker from his assets does not constitute a discrimination, the theory being that such bonds are represented by deposits rather than the invested capital of the banker.[77]

A second fertile source of discriminations has been the deduction of debts from the credits of a tax payer, a practice rather generally permitted by state laws. Do such deductions constitute a discrimination against the holders of national bank stock? The answer of the court has not been an unequivocal affirmative. In *People* v. *Weaver*,[78] the court held that the New York law, which refused to permit a stockholder of a national bank the privilege of deducting his debts from the value of his bank shares, was in conflict with Section 5219. Other cases support this general position[79] but there are qualifications of note. Deductions of debts by private, unincorporated bankers are not a discrimination as the net assets of the banker are still taxed and the deductions do not prevent substantial equality with bank shares.[80] Nor was the deduction of debts from credits, unknown in amount, held to be a violation of Section 5219 as the court was unable to say whether the inequality was substantial.[81] Again, the fact that the

[76] *Van Allen* v. *The Assessors*, 3 Wall 573 (1865); *Bradley* v. *The People*, 4 Wall 459 (1866); *Montana National Bank of Billings* v. *Yellowstone County*, 276 U. S. 499 (1928).

[77] *Des Moines National Bank* v. *Fairweather*, 263 U. S. 103 (1923).

[78] *People* v. *Weaver*, 100 U. S. 539 (1879).

[79] *Supervisors* v. *Stanley*, 105 U. S. 305 (1881); *Hills* v. *Exchange Bank*, 105 U. S. 319 (1881); *Evansville Bank* v. *Britton*, 105 U. S. 322 (1881); *Boyer* v. *Boyer*, 113 U. S. 689 (1885); *Whitbeck* v. *Mercantile National Bank of Cleveland*, 127 U. S. 193 (1888); *Lander* v. *Mercantile Bank*, 186 U. S. 458 (1902).

[80] *Des Moines National Bank* v. *Fairweather*, 263 U. S. 103 (1923).

[81] *National Bank of Wellington* v. *Chapman*, 173 U. S. 205 (1899).

law in Kansas permitted *some debts* to be deducted from *some credits,* while there was a large and important class of moneyed capital from which debts were not deductible, did not establish, in the absence of positive proof, the existence of a discrimination against holders of national bank shares who were not permitted such deductions.[82]   The fact that the Supreme Court of Kansas had previously ruled that bank shares were not credits within the meaning of the Kansas statute received judicial cognizance in the decision.   A New York law which imposed a tax of 1.0 per cent on national bank shares, with no deductions of debts allowed therefrom, while other personal property was taxed at general property rates of 1.6 per cent, with allowances for debts, was held valid in the absence of proof showing actual discrimination.[83] Finally, the court held that the Utah Supreme Court, in refusing to permit debt deductions from bank shares, was not in violation of Section 5219 since the local court had held that shares of stock were not credits within the meaning of the term in that state.[84] Consequently, the refusal of the state to permit shareholders of national banks to deduct their debts from the value of these shares, while permitting individuals to deduct such obligations from their credits, may not produce discriminations against such shares, the issue being contingent upon the legal status of such credits and shares in the individual state.   That credits are, for the most part, moneyed capital in the hands of individual citizens can scarcely be doubted.   In those cases, therefore, where the court has modified its position as to the effect of such deductions on the tax on national bank shares, either legal categories have failed to coincide with financial realities or proof of substantial inequalities has been lacking.

The absence or presence of discrimination, in the final analysis,

[82] *First National Bank of Garnett* v. *Ayers,* 160 U. S. 660 (1896) ; see also *First National Bank of Wellington* v. *Chapman,* 173 U. S. 205 (1899).
[83] *Amoskeag Savings Bank* v. *Purdy,* 231 U. S. 373 (1913).
[84] *Commercial Bank* v. *Chambers,* 182 U. S. 556 (1901).

turns on the question of the relative amount of competitive moneyed capital which is accorded a privileged tax position by the state. In *Hepburn v. The School Directors,* the amount of exempt moneyed capital was not material,[85] while in *Boyer v. Boyer,* a case involving a similar legal situation, the court held that a discrimination existed since the amount involved was admittedly large. The rule of substantial competition has been consistently affirmed in the later cases coming before the court.[86] But simple averment of competition is not sufficient to establish discrimination. The competition of other moneyed capital must be shown and the moneyed capital identified.[87]

As indicative of what inequalities have constituted discriminations, the following instances may be cited. In *Whitbeck v. Mercantile National Bank of Cleveland*[88] the court held that the equalized assessment of the shares of this bank at 65 per cent of their value, while other moneyed capital was assessed at 60 per cent in that county and in twelve other counties, constituted a

[85] See also *Adams v. Nashville,* 92 U. S. 19 (1877); *Evansville Bank v. Britton,* 105 U. S. 322 (1881).

[86] *Boyer v. Boyer,* 113 U. S. 689 (1885); *Mercantile Bank v. New York,* 121 U. S. 138 (1887); *Bank of Redemption v. Boston,* 125 U. S. 60 (1888); *Davenport Bank v. Davenport Board of Equalization,* 123 U. S. 83 (1887); *Whitbeck v. Mercantile National Bank of Cleveland,* 127 U. S. 193 (1888); *First National Bank of Garnett v. Ayers,* 160 U. S. 660 (1896); *Bank of Commerce v. Seattle,* 166 U. S. 463 (1897); *First National Bank of Wellington v. Chapman,* 173 U. S. 205 (1899); *Jenkins v. Neff,* 176 U. S. 230 (1902); *Clement National Bank v. State of Vermont,* 231 U. S. 120 (1913); *Merchants' National Bank of Richmond v. Richmond,* 256 U. S. 635 (1921); *First National Bank of Guthrie Center v. Anderson,* 269 U. S. 341 (1926); *First National Bank of Hartford v. Hartford,* 273 U. S. 548 (1927); *Georgetown National Bank v. McFarland,* 273 U. S. 568 (1927); *Minnesota v. First National Bank of St. Paul,* 273 U. S. 561 (1927).

[87] *Hills v. Exchange Bank,* 105 U. S. 319 (1881); *Aberdeen v. Chehalis County,* 166 U. S. 440 (1897); *Bank of Commerce v. Seattle,* 166 U. S. 463 (1897); *Commercial Bank v. Chambers,* 182 U. S. 556 (1901); *Amoskeag Savings Bank v. Purdy,* 231 U. S. 373 (1913).

[88] *Whitbeck v. Mercantile Bank of Cleveland,* 127 U. S. 193 (1888).

discrimination against the bank. But in *Albuquerque Bank* v. *Perea*,[89] the fact that the bank was assessed at 85 per cent of its full value and other property at 70 per cent did not constitute a discrimination when this did not come from any design or systematic effort on the part of county officials.[90] In *San Francisco Bank* v. *Dodge,* the court held that the assessment of state banks on their property and franchise did not take into account all the intangible elements of value and was therefore discriminatory against national banks whose shares were assessed at market.[91]

The court has not established any objective standard indicative of what amounts of moneyed capital constitute substantial competition, but has followed the practice of deciding in each individual case whether the competition, as shown, possessed the requisite degree of substantiality to be violative of Section 5219.

In the Richmond case the existence of tax privileged bonds, notes, and other evidences of indebtedness amounting to $6,250,-000 as compared to national bank shares with an aggregate value of $8,000,000 constituted substantial competition and therefore was discriminatory. Again, the fact that there were moneys and credits in Guthrie County amounting to approximately $5,000,000, which were taxed at the rate of five mills, while the total value of state and national bank shares taxed at general property rates in the county did not exceed $316,852 constituted a discrimination.[92]

Perhaps the most significant comparison which may be made is

[89] *Albuquerque Bank* v. *Perea,* 147 U. S. 87 (1892). Compare with the ruling in *Supervisors* v. *Stanly,* 105 U. S. 305 (1881), where the court stated that if "it can be proved that the assessors habitually and intentionally, or by some rule prescribed by themselves, or by some one whom they were bound to obey, assessed the shares of the national banks higher in proportion to their actual value than other moneyed capital generally, then there is ground for recovery."

[90] *Albuquerque Bank* v. *Perea,* 147 U. S. 87 (1892).

[91] *San Francisco Bank* v. *Dodge,* 197 U. S. 70 (1905).

[92] *First National Bank of Guthrie Center* v. *Anderson,* 269 U. S. 341 (1926).

that of the Wisconsin[93] and Minnesota[94] decisions with the Georgetown Bank case,[95] all of which were delivered on the same day. Data in the Wisconsin case showed that real estate firms operating in the vicinity of the plaintiff's bank loaned annually between $250,000 to $300,000; that various individuals, partnerships, and corporations were engaged in buying and selling notes, bonds and mortgages in that area; and that other firms located in Chicago and Milwaukee were similarly engaged, one of these firms having sold a portion of some $25,000,000 of bonds and securities in that locality. Such a situation constituted substantial competition, and since these items were exempt from property taxation and bank shares were taxed at the full property rate, a discrimination existed.

In the Minnesota case moneys and credits were listed for taxation to the amounts of $830,000,000 in the county, and $400,-000,000 in the city, where the bank was situated. Individuals had returned for taxation in Ramsey County promissory notes totalling $2,480,446 and bonds amounting to $7,595,975. Furthermore, note brokers operating in the state loaned funds amounting to $100,000,000. Cattle loan brokers also handled $22,000,000 of cattle loan paper, $13,000,000 of which was sold to banks, corporations, and firms in the state. It was further shown that national banks in Minnesota had invested in real estate mortgages to the amount of $19,000,000, in United States bonds, $41,000,-000, and in other securities, $33,800,000. Since intangibles, other than tax exempt bonds, were taxed at a three mill rate and bank shares at the full property rate, and since the evidence convinced the court of substantial competition, a discrimination existed against national bank shares.

A contrary decision was rendered, however, in the George-

[93] *First National Bank of Hartford, Wisconsin*, v. *City of Hartford*, 273 U. S. 548 (1927).
[94] *Minnesota* v. *First National Bank of St. Paul*, 273 U. S. 561 (1927).
[95] *Georgetown National Bank* v. *McFarland*, 273 U. S. 568 (1927).

town Bank case. The facts here alleged were that there were 205 individual citizens in Scott County who had invested over $1,060,000 in mortgages and purchase money notes, at least half of this amount being in the hands of money lenders. Two witnesses professed to know ten parties who loaned $122,300 to twenty-six borrowers in the county on notes of bankable grade. It was further averred that national banks in the county had invested over $800,000 in real estate mortgages. But the court held that evidence was not conclusive of discrimination.[96] The extremely able brief presented by the defendant-in-error no doubt played an important rôle in this decision, though it is patent that the factual evidence submitted was not as imposing as in the two preceding cases. It does compare favorably with the data presented in *First National Bank of Guthrie Center* v. *Anderson.*[97]

Not only has the court refused to establish objective criteria of substantial competition, but it has also been hesitant to indicate the exact area of competition.[98] It is not necessary in establishing the fact of competition to

show that national banks and competing investors solicit the same customers for the same loans or investments. It is enough as stated if both engage in seeking and securing in the same locality capital investments of the class now under consideration which are substantial in amount.

.   .   .   .

Competition may exist between other moneyed capital and capital invested in national banks, serious in character and therefore well within the purpose of Section 5219, even though the competition be with some but not all phases of the business of national banks.[99]

The court in this case expressed alarm for the safety of national banks when subjected to the competition from tax-favored

[96] *Georgetown National Bank* v. *McFarland,* 273 U. S. 570 (1927).

[97] *First National Bank of Guthrie Center* v. *Anderson,* 269 U. S. 341 (1926).

[98] *Whitbeck* v. *Mercantile National Bank,* 127 U. S. 193 (1888).

[99] *First National Bank of Hartford, Wisconsin,* v. *City of Hartford,* 273 U. S. 548, 559, 557 (1927).

specialized financial institutions. But, recently, the court, with a change in personnel, viewed the situation more realistically and discovered no discrimination in the Louisiana law which did not tax building and loan associations, auto-finance companies, Morris Plan and Morgan Plan banks, real estate mortgage, investments, and bond brokers on a parity with national banks.[100] Here the court referred to the basic differences between national banks which operate largely with deposits, and financial institutions which make loans mainly from funds secured otherwise than by deposits. Emphasis was also accorded the fact that some of the institutions handle unbankable paper. The fact that industrial, railroad, and public utility bonds were by law assessed at 10 per cent of market value did not establish a discrimination against bank shares in this instance. It is submitted that the court was here concerned not only with the way in which allegedly competing funds were being employed, but it properly took cognizance of "the character of those who compete" as well as the essential nature of the banking process. While shades of distinction, thus closely drawn, are easily subject to over-emphasis, one can but conclude that there is in this pronouncement a much clearer analysis of the issues involved and a much more realistically defensible position assumed. Who can deny that deposit banking and specialized financial institutions, while unquestionably competitive in certain areas of their operations, are, however, substantially different in their financial functions?

The existence of substantial competition, in the final analysis, is a matter of subjective determination by the court in each case, in the establishment of which both the facts presented and the relative skill of the counsels play an important rôle. That the court gives careful consideration to the factual evidence cannot be questioned, but it is also true that the absence of objective

[100] *First National Bank of Shreveport* v. *Louisiana Tax Commission,* 289 U. S. 60 (1933).

standards of substantial competition forces the court not infrequently to such general defenses as "the evidence as a whole" or "the spirit of the law" or "the intent to discriminate." In other cases instances of actual competition are cited and analyzed.

Such a policy makes the status of national bank taxation uncertain and unpredictable. It is not unique in the realm of law as its counterpart may be found in the law of criminal conspiracy, secondary boycotts, sympathetic strikes, and picketing. To an extent such a condition is irremediable, but the court has at times complicated the bank tax situation by adopting a conception of competition which, when viewed from the standpoint of economic reality, approaches the realm of absurdity. How, for example, could the operations of individual investors be declared to be competitive with the business of national banks when the court had so much trouble in determining the status of trust companies, or when insurance companies, which hold millions of dollars of securities of the types banks buy, are excluded from the realm of competition? How real is the competition of individuals in their investment operations with national banks, when these operators do not have to solicit the same customers? It is illuminating to compare the court's former conception with that of the Federal Reserve Board which is required, under the Clayton Act, to determine when two national banks are in substantial competition in order to prevent interlocking directorates. The board says:

In general . . . two banks . . . would be deemed to be in substantial competition . . . if the business engaged in by such banks under natural and normal conditions conflicts or interferes, or if the cessation of competition between the two would be injurious to customers or would-be customers, or would result in appreciably lessening the volume of business or kinds of business of either institution. . . . Two banks engaged in the same character of business . . . would be in substantial competition if their fields of activity extended over the same geographical territory. . . . Again, if they conducted their operations in the same place, but because of their comparatively small size in relation to the total banking opportunities of the locality, and because of the fact that they did not deal with the same class of customers . . . they would not necessarily be deemed in substantial competition. Or, if their operations were conducted in the same locality, but the character of business engaged in differs fundamentally (for example, where one does only an essentially commercial banking business, while the other does only an essentially trust-company or fiduciary business), such banks need not be regarded as in substantial competition.[101]

In the Louisiana case the court has more nearly approached the above interpretation. It remains to be seen whether this position will be maintained.

It may also be suggested that the court might examine the fiscal effects of low rates on competing intangibles in the determination of discriminations against banks as the circuit court did in *National Bank* v. *Baltimore*.[102] Where the assessment of intangibles at low millage rates results in increased revenues from this source by eliciting larger aggregate assessments, other tax payers, including national banks, are benefited rather than prejudiced. Such a position would take cognizance of financial realities as well as legal categories. So long as the court looks only to the latter, and the states are forced to tax intangibles at general property rates in order to validate share taxation of national banks, these intangibles will indubitably be driven to cover.

Experience at this point is conclusive. Immediately following the Richmond decision a number of states, among them New York and Iowa, sought to circumvent the effect of this decision by classing competing moneyed capital with bank shares for tax purposes while other intangibles were either taxable at low rates

[101] *Federal Reserve Bulletin*, II, 390 ff. For an excellent discussion of this consideration, see Lutz, "Evolution of Section 5219," *Bul.*, N. T. A. XIII, 260 ff.

[102] *National Bank of Baltimore* v. *Mayor of Baltimore*, 100 Fed. 23 (1900).

or exempt from property levies.[103]   In such cases it was left to the tax officials to ferret out the competing moneyed capital.   The administration of the law in New York resulted in appeals to the state courts to identify the other moneyed capital.   The decisions were not satisfactory to the national banks and the issue was carried to the federal court, the banks contending that the tax officials, acting under the interpretations of the New York court, had not in fact assessed taxable competing moneyed capital.   A very exhaustive brief showing the existence of such non-assessed capital led to a decision favorable to the banks in the lower courts which was sustained by the United States Supreme Court in a memorandum decision.[104]   Thus, the position was taken that competing moneyed capital, when legally taxable at the rate applied to national bank shares, must *in fact,* be so assessed or the bank tax is null *in toto.*

A somewhat similar case, arising in Iowa, was also favorable to the banks.   In this instance competing moneyed capital was taxable at general property rates, as were also bank shares, but the assessor had wrongfully listed the competing moneyed capital as moneys and credits, taxable at five mills.   The Iowa court held that the act of the assessor was usurpative and without the authority of the state and hence did not create a discrimination.   The United States Supreme Court reversed the Iowa court.[105]   With respect to the state bank involved in this case, the discrimination rested wholly on the equal protection clause of the Fourteenth Amendment in so far as any federal right was involved.   The counsel for the bank in *Union Bank and Trust Company* v. *Phelps,* in a later case from Alabama, relied heavily on the above

[103] See chap. 5, *infra.*

[104] *Keating et al.* v. *The Public National Bank,* 284 U. S. 578 (1931). For the nature of the evidence see, *Brief for Appellee, Keating* v. *Public National Bank.*

[105] *Iowa-Des Moines National Bank* v. *Bennett et al.,* 284 U. S. 239 (1931).

decision in seeking to nullify the share taxes on state banks following the invalidity of the same on national banks, but the court held that the classification of state banks for tax purposes was, in this instance, valid.[106]

In view of these decisions, it would appear that to validate the share tax on national banks, the competing moneyed capital, when legally taxable at the rate applied to such shares, must *in fact* be so taxed. It is not certain, however, that state banks can successfully invoke the protection of the federal statute in such situations in the light of *Union Bank and Trust Company* v. *Phelps*. Since human ingenuity has as yet failed to devise any method by which competing moneyed capital can be fully assessed, it is obvious that national banks, and perhaps state banks as well, may completely annul their share taxes by a clever assembling of data showing a substantial volume of undertaxed or non-assessed competing moneyed capital even if, legally, such capital is taxable at the rate applicable to bank shares.

Discriminations against national bank shares are not restricted merely to the privileged treatment of state banks and moneyed capital. In those states in which the several constitutions require the uniform taxation of all property, discriminations against banks may arise as a result of the undertaxation of other property. In *Cummings* v. *National Bank*[107] the court held that the assessment of real estate at one-third its value constituted a violation of the uniformity provision of the Ohio constitution, and the banks by paying taxes on one-third of the value of their shares had fulfilled their tax liabilities.

The effect of discriminations on the status of the state law presents another interesting problem. If the discrimination is against a particular class of national bank shareholders rather

[106] *Union Bank and Trust Company* v. *Phelps*, 288 U. S. 181 (1933). See chap. 9, *infra*.

[107] *Cummings* v. *National Bank*, 101 U. S. 153 (1879).

than against all stockholders, the law is not wholly invalid. State statutes which did not permit the deduction of debts from national bank shares, while permitting such deductions from other credits, were voidable only to the shareholders who had legally established such debts and merely to the extent of the assessed value of their shares which were offset by these obligations.[108] Discriminations against all stockholders of the same national bank, occasioned by the assessment of the shares at a higher percentage of their value than other assessed personal property, did not invalidate the assessment *in toto* but only that amount which was in excess of the percentage applied to other property.[109]

When the discrimination against national bank shares arose from the imposition of different nominal rates of taxation on such shares and other moneyed capital, the court has not been so meticulous. The taxation of bonds and other evidences of debt in Virginia at a combined state and municipal rate of 95 cents per $100, while bank shares were taxed at a combined rate of $1.75, constituted an obvious discrimination which invalidated the state law and city ordinance imposing the tax in so far as national bank shares were concerned.[110] In like manner, the taxation of intangibles in Iowa[111] at five mills and in Minnesota[112] at three mills per dollar, when national bank shares were taxed at the general property rate, rendered the assessment of national bank shares completely void. In these later cases the position of the court has been that the statutes themselves were in conflict with Section 5219 and therefore void as to such shares, since a dis-

[108] *People* v. *Weaver,* 100 U. S. 539 (1879); *Supervisors* v. *Stanly,* 105 U. S. 305 (1881); *Hills* v. *Exchange Bank,* 105 U. S. 319 (1881); *Evansville Bank* v. *Britton,* 105 U. S. 322 (1881); *Whitbeck* v. *Mercantile National Bank,* 127 U. S. 193 (1888).

[109] *Whitbeck* v. *Mercantile National Bank,* 127 U. S. 193 (1888).

[110] *Merchants' National Bank* v. *Richmond,* 256 U. S. 635 (1921).

[111] *First National Bank of Guthrie Center* v. *Anderson,* 269 U. S. 341 (1926).

[112] *Minnesota* v. *First National Bank of St. Paul,* 273 U. S. 561 (1927).

crimination was implicit on the face of the statute. For similar reasons the taxation of national bank shares at general property rates was invalid in Wisconsin when other moneyed capital, exempt from property taxation, was taxed on the income therefrom.[113]

In opposition to this view it may be suggested that, in so ruling, the court may have disregarded the principle that the rate of taxation has reference to the tax burden on such banks and other moneyed capital, in which case only the excess of the tax on bank shares was invalid. The Supreme Court of Massachusetts took this position, the court holding that the taxation of bank shares at the rate of $28.48 per $1000, when only the income from intangibles was taxed at 6 per cent, did not entirely invalidate the tax on national bank shares.[114] But in this issue the Supreme Court of Massachusetts is not supreme.

There remains yet to be considered the court's interpretation of the constitutional status of Section 5219. It will be recalled that the court in *McCulloch* v. *Maryland* took the position that Maryland had original power to tax the interest of its citizens in the Second United States Bank. It will also be remembered that Congress, in its debate on the tax provisions of the National Bank Act, discussed the constitutionality of the issue at considerable length, and its final solution was in line with the *dicta* of the court.[115] The position of the court and the attitude of Congress point to the conclusion that the taxation of bank shares was a power resident in the sovereignty of the states.

If this position had been maintained by the court in its later decisions, many problems, which became the source of great vexation to tax officials and the court itself, might easily have been avoided. Instead, it resorted to inconsistent interpretations of the

[113] *First National Bank of Hartford, Wisconsin,* v. *Hartford,* 273 U. S. 548 (1927).

[114] *Central National Bank* v. *Lynn,* 156 N. E. 42 (1927).

[115] See chap. 2, *supra.*

nature and source of the power which the states exercised in the taxation of national bank shares.[116]

In *Van Allen* v. *The Assessors,* the court recognized the original power of taxation vested in the states, but asserted that Congress and the states had concurrent powers over certain subjects, and by virtue of the paramount authority of Congress it could permit or exclude the state from the exercise of such concurrent power. State taxation of the means and instruments of the federal government fell into this category.[117]

The extent to which federal agencies are subject to taxation by the state is indicated in a later decision in which the court, in discussing the proposition that the power to tax may be the power to destroy, observes:

The principle we are discussing has its limitation, a limitation growing out of the necessity on which the principle itself is founded. *That limitation is, that the agencies of the Federal government are only exempted from State legislation, so far as that legislation may interfere with, or impair their efficiency in performing the functions by which they are designed to serve that government.* Any other rule would convert a principle founded alone in the necessity of exercising the legitimate powers, into an unauthorized and unjustifiable invasion of the rights of the States.[118]

Applying this general principle in 1876 to a Vermont law which required national banks to provide assessing officers with certain pertinent data, the court held that such a provision was not an infringement of the functions of these federal agencies. The position of the court is stated as follows:

. . . *We have more than once held in this Court that the national banks organized under the Acts of Congress are subject to State*

[116] See A. J. Schweppe, "State Taxation of National Bank Stock," *Minnesota Law Review,* VI, 219 ff.; Henry Rottschaefer, "State Taxation of National Bank Shares," *Minnesota Law Review,* VII, 357 ff.; R. J. Traynor, "National Bank Taxation," *California Law Review,* XVII, 83 ff.

[117] *Van Allen v. The Assessors,* 3 Wall 573 (1865).

[118] *National Bank v. Commonwealth,* 9 Wall 353, 362 (1869). Italics by the writer.

legislation, except where such legislation is in conflict with some act of Congress, or where it tends to impair or destroy the utility of such banks, as agents or instrumentalities of the United States, or interferes with the purposes of their creation."[119]

It would appear, therefore, that the states may tax national bank shares, by virtue of their original power of taxation, only to the extent that Congress and the court hold such taxation to be free from any essential impairment of the functions which these banks were designed to perform.

From the theory that the states had original power to tax national bank shares, the court shifted to the view that the power of the states to tax national banks was the result of a direct grant by Congress. The distance between these opinions was not negotiated in one leap. The court in *Farmers' and Mechanics National Bank* v. *Dearing*,[120] in discussing the constitutionality of Section 5219, classified the powers of government as follows: (1) those belonging exclusively to the states; (2) those belonging exclusively to the national government; (3) those which may be exercised concurrently and independently by both; and (4) those which may be exercised by the states but only with the consent, express or implied, of Congress. The power of the states to tax national banks, continued the court, belongs to the last named, and whenever the will of the nation intervenes exclusively in this class of cases, the authority of the state retires and lies in abeyance until a proper occasion for its exercise shall recur, the federal law being supreme. State taxation of national banks is exercised, therefore, solely by consent of Congress.

This, however, does not represent the final position of the court. Just four years later the court held that the power of state taxation of national banks arises solely from Section 5219, which

[119] *Waite* v. *Dowley*, 94 U. S. 527, 532-33 (1876). Italics by the writer.
[120] *Farmers' and Mechanics National Bank* v. *Dearing*, 91 U. S. 29 (1875).

provision was necessary to authorize the states to impose any tax whatsoever on these bank shares. The court said:

As Congress was conferring a power on the States which they would not otherwise have had, to tax these shares, it undertook to impose a restriction on the exercise of that power, manifestly designed to prevent taxation which should discriminate against this class of property as compared with other moneyed capital.[121]

By judicial fiat the power of the state to tax national bank shares is thus conferred by Congress on the states; without such a direct grant the states would be impotent. How far this decision may be harmonized with the *dictum* of the Van Allen case in which it was stated that the states were not capable of receiving such a grant of authority, even if Congress had the power to confer it, which in the mind of the court it did not have, is not clear to the layman.

However, the solution of this judicial skein is no more difficult than the position next taken in *Talbott* v. *Silver Bow County,*[122] in which case the court stated that national bank shares were taxable by states solely by the consent of Congress, and then proceeded to justify this position upon the *dicta* of Chief Justice Marshall in *McCulloch* v. *Maryland,* and *Osborn* v. *Bank of the United States,* using the distinguished Justice's logic, but overlooking entirely the qualifications there made relating to the taxation of real estate and the interest of the citizens of the state in the federal bank. The court here contends that the state taxation of national banks, their property, assets, or franchise rests solely upon the permissive legislation of Congress. This position it has maintained in its later decisions.[123]

[121] *People* v. *Weaver,* 100 U. S. 539, 543 (1879). Italics by the writer.
[122] *Talbott* v. *Silver Bow County,* 139 U. S. 438 (1891).
[123] *Owensboro National Bank* v. *Owensboro,* 173 U. S. 664 (1899); *Home Savings Bank* v. *City of Des Moines,* 205 U. S. 503 (1907); *Bank of California* v. *Richardson,* 248 U. S. 476 (1919); *Des Moines National Bank* v. *Fairweather,* 263 U. S. 103 (1923); *First National Bank of Guthrie Center* v. *Anderson,* 269 U. S. 341 (1926).

As the later position of the court is inconsistent with its former attitude, the probable interpretation which it would now make if it were confronted with a case turning solely upon the constitutionality of the national bank share tax is of course a matter of conjecture. It has been suggested that the court might revert to the original position taken in *McCulloch* v. *Maryland*. There are reasons to believe otherwise. Since the issue of the taxation of federal agencies is not covered by an express provision in the federal Constitution, the doctrine of immunity from taxation was first enunciated by the court as a reasonable hypothesis to meet a concrete situation. The court does not, however, consider itself the sole arbiter of the extent to which the federal government may waive immunity from the state taxation of its agencies. It has held that Congress may exercise, within certain limits, its discretion in such matters. Evidence of this fact is seen in the position of the court with respect to the taxation of obligations of the federal government, payable upon demand. In 1868 the court held that United States notes, payable upon demand and receivable for all public dues, though they were intended by Congress to circulate as money, were, nevertheless, obligations of the federal government and exempt from state taxation.[124] In this case the court said:

We think it clearly within the discretion of Congress to determine whether, in view of the circumstances attending the issue of the notes, their usefulness, as a means of carrying on the government, would be enhanced by exemption from taxation; and within the constitutional power of Congress, having resolved the question of usefulness affirmatively, to provide law for such exemption.[125]

Congress, in 1894, authorized the state taxation of national bank notes, and other notes and certificates of the federal government, payable upon demand, subject to the restriction that the rate

[124] *Bank v. Supervisors,* 7 Wall 26 (1868).
[125] *Ibid.,* pp. 30 ff.

and manner of taxation should be the same as for other money.[126]
The waiving of this exemption from taxation by Congress received judicial cognizance in *Hibernia Savings Society* v. *San
Francisco* in a case involving the liability to state taxation of
checks drawn by the Treasurer of the United States and payable
upon demand within four months. The checks were the property
of the bank, having been drawn in payment of the interest on
United States securities held by the bank. The court held these
checks to be taxable despite the fact that they were obligations of
the United States which were not intended to circulate as money.
The court cited the federal statute of 1894, and said:

> Although the checks in question were not intended to circulate as
> money, and therefore do not fall within the letter of the statute, the
> reasons that apply to that class of obligations we think apply with
> equal force to checks intended for immediate payment, though not
> intended to circulate as money.[127]

It is conceivable, therefore, that the court would recognize as
valid the proper exercise of the discretion of Congress on the
matter of waiving, or removing the waiver of, immunity of national banks from state taxation, so long as such taxation does not
hinder them in the efficient exercise of their proper powers and
does not prevent them from discharging their functions as federal
agencies. If this view be correct, the conclusion is reached that
Congress has the constitutional power to determine the manner
and extent of the taxation of national banks within the limits of
the theory of national sovereignty.[128]

[126] *United States Statutes at Large*, XXVIII, 278.

[127] *Hibernia Savings Society* v. *San Francisco*, 200 U. S. 310, 316
(1906).

[128] An interesting parallel case arose in Australia in which the court
there held that the Commonwealth may authorize state taxation of federal
salaries previously held invalid without such authority. See *Chaplin* v.
Commissioner, 12 Comm. Law Rep. 375 (Australia, 1911).

CHAPTER IV

THE AMENDMENTS OF 1923 AND 1926 TO
SECTION 5219

WHILE Section 5219 was subjected to frequent interpretation, no statutory changes were made in its provisions
until 1923 save only the amendment of 1868. The absence of
legislation does not imply that the groups directly involved were
satisfied with the status of bank taxation which it enforced. The
law confined the state taxation of national banks to levies on the
real property and the shares, which, if fully assessed, tended to
exact heavier taxes from banks than were imposed on other property.[1] The bankers in 1920 expressed the desire for an amendment which would circumscribe the area of judicial interpretation
and set definite limits on bank taxation.[2] Then came the Richmond decision[3] which clearly imperilled the share taxes in some
eighteen classified property tax states and in twelve other states
which exempted competing moneyed capital from the property tax
but subjected the income therefrom to an income tax.[4] Even in
the general property tax states particular provisions, such as the
exemption of mortgages or the deduction of debts from credits,
rendered share taxation vulnerable to litigation.

It soon became apparent that the bankers would capitalize this
advantage. In New York a large number of suits were launched,
over 100 claims being filed within six months after the Richmond

[1] *Proceedings,* National Tax Association, 1919, pp. 449 ff.

[2] American Bankers Association Supplement, *Commercial and Financial
Chronicle,* 1920, pp. 155 ff.

[3] *Merchants' National Bank of Richmond* v. *City of Richmond,* 256
U. S. 635 (1921).

[4] *Hearings* before the Committee on Banking and Currency of the
House of Representatives on H. R. 9579, 67th Cong., 2d sess., 1922, pp.
64 ff.

decision.[5] The city comptroller of New York estimated that
$20,000,000 of taxes would be lost as a result of a decision favor-
able to the bankers. In Boston four suits involving $2,528,000
of taxes were filed.[6] In North Dakota the national banks refused
to pay the taxes imposed on them for the years 1919, 1920 and
1921.[7] The validity of the tax on national bank stock in Wisconsin was also challenged. The movement to nullify bank taxes
was rapidly spreading.

Meanwhile, alarmed tax officials inaugurated a movement to
amend Section 5219. The National Tax Association in 1921
suggested an amendment which would permit the states to tax
either the shares or the income of national banks subject to the
restriction that the burden imposed should not be heavier than
that levied on capital invested in the banking business or the income derived therefrom. In December, 1921, representatives
from sixteen states drew up a bill embodying these features which
was introduced on December 15, 1921, as H. R. 9579.[8] It further
provided that the income from dividends on bank shares could be
taxed to the stockholder under the personal income tax. It sought
also to validate all taxes on national banks imposed under existing
state laws. Hearings were held by the House committee on January 25-27 and February 7-9, 1922, at which both the tax officials
and the bankers presented their views as to the amendment of
Section 5219. Prior to and during the hearings, futile attempts
were made in conferences to iron out the differences between
these groups.[9]

The arguments of the tax authorities for the bill emphasized
the effect of changed conditions on the position of national banks.
Recalling the fact that the National Bank Act was in part a
product of the Civil War, it was urged that the protection which

[5] *Ibid.*, p. 32.   [8] *Proc.* N. T. A., 1922, p. 250.
[6] *Ibid.*, p. 12.   [9] House *Hearings,* 1922, pp. 102, 113 ff.
[7] *Ibid.*, p. 38.

Section 5219 insured these institutions from the then-existing prejudices and hostility of state banks, state legislatures, and states-rights enthusiasts was no longer necessary to safeguard national banks from discriminatory treatment.[10] Cognizance was taken of the fact that financial institutions had undergone remarkable changes during these sixty years.[11] State banks and trust companies had largely supplanted the individual lender as significant competitors of national banks. The corporation had become general and intangible property was a commonplace. The dismal failure of the general property tax to reach effectively intangible property had resulted in the adoption of classification and income taxation as more effective methods of taxing intangible wealth.[12] To continue Section 5219, as now interpreted by the court, would force those states to surrender these superior methods of taxation which in some states had been espoused by the bankers to their own benefit.[13] The only other alternative would be to forego the taxation of national banks. Section 5219 thus appeared to block the road to progressive tax reform.

Moreover, it was contended that Section 5219 lacked clarity and precision, its meaning being contingent upon the construction of the court in each case. By a process of judicial interpretation, it had been whittled down until the tax systems of numerous states, originally thought to rest on secure legal foundations, had been endangered by the vagaries of the Richmond decision.[14] It was, therefore, imperative that a statute be passed which, while lacking nothing in justice, would insure certainty and precision in bank taxation. The bill as proposed was said to meet these requirements.[15] Consequently, it had the unanimous support of

[10] *Ibid.*, pp. 99, 104, 226.
[11] *Ibid.*, p. 246.
[12] *Ibid.*, pp. 5, 11, 64, 65, 82, 208, 247.
[13] *Ibid.*, pp. 5, 7, 175, 243.
[14] *Ibid.*, pp. 20, 21, 65, 91, 95, 100, 173, 203, 208, 213, 227.
[15] *Ibid.*, pp. 21, 92, 102, 106.

the states.[16] Finally, it was emphasized that immediate amendment was necessary. The multiplication of suits and the threatened heavy losses in state and local revenues would paralyze local finances, embarrass seriously local governments, and disrupt systems of state taxation.[17]

The position assumed by the bankers was one of opposition to the bill. They were willing to permit the states to tax the income of national banks as an alternate to share taxation, but insisted upon the retention of the other moneyed capital limit.[18] Accordingly, they proposed a bill embodying these features.[19] The chief argument advanced by the bankers against H. R. 9579 was that it permitted the segregation of banks for purposes of state taxation with no effective limits on the taxes which the states might impose on them. They insisted that such a classification would encourage the discriminatory taxation of all banks.[20] The tax experience of bankers was convincing that there was a pronounced tendency for the states to seize unfairly upon them as a facile source of revenue,[21] a tendency which was intensified by the widespread prejudice against banks and the general ignorance as to the nature of their operations.[22] Banks, segregated for tax purposes, would be politically impotent to prevent such discriminations owing to the small number of people injuriously affected as opposed to the large number of beneficiaries. Therefore, Section 5219, as it stood, was an essential bulwark of protection against tax discriminations,[23] not only to national banks but for state banks as well.[24]

[16] *Ibid.*, p. 91.
[17] *Ibid.*, pp. 13, 15, 46, 95.
[18] *Ibid.*, p. 113.
[19] *Ibid.*, p. 114.
[20] *Ibid.*, pp. 117, 121, 126, 139, 148, 155, 163, 184, 195, 210.
[21] *Ibid.*, pp. 121, 126, 163, 184, 195. See chap. 9, *infra.*
[22] House *Hearings,* 1922, pp. 119 ff.
[23] *Ibid.*, pp. 111-113, 140.
[24] *Ibid.*, p. 112.

The bankers insisted, moreover, that the proposed change would give tax preference to important private bankers, such as J. P. Morgan, and others who came into competition with national banks.[25] It was pointed out that there were 799 private bankers in the United States in 1920, with assets totaling $212,626,000,[26] and it was asserted that $1,700,000,000 of "other moneyed capital" in New York alone was not taxed.[27] Likewise, there were note brokers engaged in competition with national banks whose business ran into enormous sums. It was urged that the taxation of such firms only on income, while national banks were subjected to heavy share taxation, was an open invitation to those firms to drive national banks out of existence.

It was argued that Congress, in protecting national banks, was also safeguarding the foundations of the Federal Reserve System in which national banks were compulsory members.[28] It was pointed out that only 7 per cent of the state banks were members of the Federal Reserve System despite the fact that every legitimate effort has been made to encourage them to join.[29] While the services performed by the Federal Reserve System cannot be minimized, it is a mistaken conception of membership to regard it as a claim for a tax preferred position. Membership carries with it many compensating advantages which the bankers, upon other occasion, are wont to extol. As a matter of fact, a number of large state banks are members, and all state banks perform a national service by providing deposit currency.

It was not the intention of the banks, so avowed their spokesmen, to evade just taxation. National banks have paid and were paying taxes more than commensurate with justice. Their willingness to pay more than they were legally compelled to pay indicated, it was urged, their sense of fiscal responsibility.

[25] *Ibid.*, pp. 37, 61 ff., 68, 132 ff.   [28] *Ibid.*, p. 43.
[26] *Ibid.*, p. 138.   [29] *Ibid.*, pp. 112, 118, 120, 169.
[27] *Ibid.*, p. 67.

Following the hearings on H. R. 9579, the Committee on Banking and Currency pigeon-holed this bill and reported one of their own, H. R. 11939.[30] The new bill was in line with the wishes of the bankers as it made no change in the share tax provision but did provide for an alternative tax on net income to the bank. The validation clause was also made innocuous as it authorized the validation of only such taxes as could be levied under the terms of the bill.[31]   Mr. Nelson of Wisconsin pointed out that the pending bill did not change the existing situation at all.   He urged the application of the test of "moneyed capital in the business of banking" instead of the retention of the "other moneyed capital" limit.[32]   Mr. Williamson of South Dakota also opposed the measure on the ground that the limit was too general and that it would put national banks in a favored tax position as contrasted with state banks.[33]   But the measure, with perfunctory attention, passed the House without a record vote on June 14, 1922.[34]

Meanwhile, the tax officials had drafted a new proposal which Senator Kellogg of Minnesota introduced on April 20, 1922, as S. 3695.[35]   It provided that the limit on the share tax should be the rate[36] "assessed upon other moneyed capital employed in the business of banking," and the limit on the alternative income tax should be the rate applied to the net income from the same source. The validation clause of the Kellogg bill permitted the states to validate any taxes previously imposed on national bank shares

[30] *Proc.*, N. T. A., 1922, p. 253.

[31] *Congressional Record*, 67th Cong., 2d sess., p. 8724.   It is impossible to say how many states were as yet affected by the validation clause.   Mr. McFadden said in the House that 27 states were involved in the situation but that few banks had paid their taxes under protest.

[32] *Ibid.*, p. 8735.

[33] *Ibid.*, p. 8733.

[34] *Ibid.*, pp. 8736, 8738.   The motion to recommit the bill was lost by a vote of 173 to 28.

[35] *Proc.*, N. T. A., 1922, p. 253.

[36] *Ibid.*, p. 254; *Eighth Report of the Minnesota Tax Commission*, p. 110.

provided such taxes were not greater than those imposed during the same period on state banks and trust companies.

The issue lagged in the Senate until Senator Kellogg announced on December 22 that he would move to discharge the sub-committee, to which the bill was referred, if it did not immediately report.[37] He emphasized the fact that such taxation of banks as existed in certain states was but the result of a gentlemen's agreement which could be upset at any time by the action of a single bank or a single stockholder. The Senate committee then proposed an amended bill which would limit the share tax to the average of the rates applied to mercantile, manufacturing, and business corporations, the purpose being to prevent the segregation of banks for purposes of taxation.[38] Senator Kellogg offered an amendment to restrict the tax to the average rate applied to the shares of such limiting corporations.[39] Thus revised, the bill passed the Senate. A validation provision, embodied in a separate bill, would legalize such taxes on national banks as had been imposed on state banks or trust companies.[40]

In these forms the respective bills were advanced to the conference committee. Conversations extending over a period of nearly two months failed of agreement.[41] Whereupon, an amendment to the House bill was offered by Mr. McFadden on February 27, just four days prior to the expiration of Congress. The time allotted for debate on the measure was two hours.[42] The amended bill provided for three alternative methods of taxation. The states could tax the net income of national banks provided the rate was not higher than that on financial corporations nor higher than the highest of the rates assessed on the net income of mercantile, manufacturing, and business corporations. Or the states could tax the net income from dividends on bank shares to the

[37] *Congressional Record,* 67th Cong., 4th sess., p. 845.
[38] *Ibid.,* p. 1455.   [39] *Ibid.,* p. 2172.
[40] *Ibid.,* pp. 2219, 2224.   [41] *Ibid.,* p. 4783.
[42] *Ibid.,* p. 4782.

stockholder provided the rate on such income was not greater than that applied to the net income from other moneyed capital. Finally, the states could employ the share tax if the rate was not greater than that assessed upon competitive moneyed capital. To this limit the following clause was added:

Provided, that bonds, notes, or other evidences of indebtedness in the hands of individual citizens not employed or engaged in the banking or investment business and representing merely personal investments not made in competition with such business, shall not be deemed moneyed capital within the meaning of this section.[43]

By this provision it was claimed that the ruling of the court in the Richmond case would be over-ruled.[44]

Opposition arose in the House both to the content of the amendment and to the way in which it was being railroaded through that body.[45] Mr. Newton of Minnesota observed that, while he had not had an opportunity to determine the feasibility of the new proposal, he did think the Senate bill was workable. He then aptly observed, "Naturally, those of us who have fought for this legislation question it when it seems to meet the approval of those who originally said, 'We do not want to see Section 5219 altered.' "[46]

Mr. Wingo of Arkansas declared that the proposed measure was not new, that it required equal taxation of all capital engaged in banking while the Senate bill did not, that it looked towards the character of the moneyed capital while the Senate bill regarded only the character of the business engaged in. He asserted that the Senate proposition was new and untried, certain to produce expensive and long continued litigation, while the House proposal offers "a tried simple rule that is well settled by a long line of judicial decisions, with such additions to it as will clearly and unequivocally overrule the Richmond decision."[47] Thus, in rapid

[43] *Ibid.,* p. 4795. [46] *Ibid.,* p. 4799.
[44] *Ibid.,* p. 4802. [47] *Ibid.,* p. 4803.
[45] *Ibid.,* pp. 4800 ff.

order and with only two copies of the bill available for the consultation of the entire House the measure was passed.

The Senate conferees had insisted that the limit on the share tax be "moneyed capital employed in the business of banking within the taxing State,"[48] but they failed to secure the support of the House conferees. So on March 1 the amended House bill was introduced in the Senate and passed.

The legislative history of the 1923 amendment to Section 5219 shows that a small coterie in the House was largely responsible for its character by refusing to accept the Senate compromise provision and by rushing through an amended bill in the closing days of Congress without permitting adequate discussion thereon, the parliamentary situation being urged as a defense for their strategy. The Senate then found itself in the position of having to take the House bill or nothing at all. If the House had really desired to amend Section 5219 in such a way as to eliminate purely private investments from the limit on national bank taxation and at the same time insure the equal taxation of private and incorporated banks, it is difficult to understand the objections to the Senate compromise. It would have excluded private investments from the measure of national bank taxation; the House provision succeeded admirably in keeping them within that limit. The bill was approved by the President on March 3, 1923.[49] Whereupon, the general counsel of the American Bankers Association was able to report that the amended law "is virtually the bill advocated by the Special Committee on Taxation of the American Bankers Association."[50]

The net result of the 1923 Amendment, viewed from the standpoint of practical tax policy, was to provide the states employing the corporate income tax with an alternative to the bank

[48] *Ibid.,* p. 4802.
[49] *Ibid.,* p. 5556.
[50] *American Bankers Association Journal,* XV, 639.

share tax. The income tax on the dividends from bank stock as personal income to the stockholder would have produced so little revenue as to make its selection by many states extremely unlikely. In fact it was never used until Vermont adopted it in 1931.[51] The original bill, H. R. 9579, had provided that states employing income taxation could tax both the net income to the bank and the dividends as personal income to the stockholder, but Congress saw fit to make them alternative methods of national bank taxation.

The 1923 Amendment was not well received by the tax authorities. It was pointed out that in practically all states employing the corporate income tax, it was supplementary to, and not a substitute for, property taxation, whereas Section 5219 made such a tax on banks exclusive.[52] Again, it was urged that the amendment instead of broadening the class of tax payers used as a measure of the share tax narrowed it, and that the phraseology employed was probably as ambiguous and indefinite as that of the original act.[53] The absolute repeal of Section 5219 was suggested as a proper step.[54] It was contended by some that national banks as incorporated institutions doing a deposit business should be subjected to higher taxation than was imposed on private holders of other moneyed capital,[55] and that the Fourteenth Amendment would provide ample protection against discriminatory taxation.[56] The fact that Section 5219 forced the states to adapt their tax systems to it and to discriminate against their own subjects and favor national banks was cited as a reason for a further modification of that statute.[57] After a long and heated discussion,

[51] *Laws of Vermont*, 1931, No. 17.
[52] J. V. Gary, "State Taxation of Banks," *Proc.*, N. T. A., 1923, p. 188.
[53] W. W. Law, "Taxation of Banks," *Proc.*, N. T. A., 1923, 211.
[54] *Proc.*, N. T. A., 1923, pp. 212 ff., 220 ff.
[55] *Ibid.*, pp. 213, 220 ff., 229, 387.
[56] *Report of State Tax Commission*, New York, 1923, pp. 30 ff.
[57] *Proc.*, N. T. A., 1923, p. 377.

the National Tax Association in 1923 passed a resolution calling for a further amendment designed to give the states the power to tax national banks subject only to such limitations as the federal Constitution imposed.[58]

The income tax alternatives provided in the 1923 Amendment did not prove attractive to the states, and in 1925 the National Tax Association authorized the appointment of a committee to confer with the committee of the American Bankers Association to the end that a suitable amendment relating solely to income taxation might be effected.[59]   This movement had its origin in the desire of the banks in Massachusetts and New York to be taxed on income rather than on shares.[60] Business corporations in New York were subjected to a franchise tax which was measured by net income.   Income from intangibles, which were not competitive with national banks, was taxed as personal income.   Since the net income of national banks and the dividends on the stock could not both be subject to taxation under the provisions of Section 5219, New York had not seen fit to relinquish its share tax on banks. The banks therefore hoped by further liberalization of the income tax provisions of that statute to make it possible to substitute income taxation for share taxation.   Massachusetts had also been experimenting with a franchise tax on banks in the effort to reach income from tax exempt sources following the invalidation of the share tax in that state.[61]

In order better to accommodate Section 5219 to the employment of such income and franchise taxation, committees representing both the bankers and the tax authorities met January 22-23, 1926, and drafted an amendment to that statute,[62] which

[58] *Ibid.*, pp. 361 ff.

[59] *Ibid.*, 1926, pp. 281 ff.; *Bul.*, N. T. A., XI, 134 f.

[60] *Proc.*, N. T. A., 1926, p. 284.

[61] Henry F. Long, "Bank and Corporation Taxes in Massachusetts," *National Municipal Review*, XIV, 470 ff.

[62] *Proc.*, N. T. A., 1926, p. 283.

with minor changes was submitted to Congress. Identical bills were introduced in the Senate and the House. The Senate passed the measure without debate, and the House acted favorably after a brief discussion, the measure having been unanimously reported by the House Committee on Banking and Currency.[63] On March 24, 1926, the bill was approved and signed by the President.[64]

Two changes were embodied in this amendment. First, the states were given a fourth alternative of imposing a franchise or excise tax, measured by net income, on national banks provided the rate imposed was not higher than that assessed on financial corporations, nor higher than the highest rate imposed on the net income of mercantile, manufacturing, and business corporations. Second, it was now made possible for a state to impose a tax on the dividend income from bank shares to the stockholder in conjunction with either the tax on net income or the franchise tax measured by net income. The fourth alternative obviously sought to make the net income from tax exempt securities taxable to the bank. Thus the states now have four alternatives each subject to specific limits: (1) a tax on shares, (2) a tax on net income to the bank, (3) a tax on the net income from dividends to the stockholder, (4) a franchise tax, measured by net income, to the bank. These are mutually exclusive methods except, as above stated, the tax on dividend income may be combined with either the corporate net income or franchise tax.[65]

While the 1926 Amendment was being negotiated, the United States Supreme Court delivered a decision interpretative of the effect of the 1923 Amendment in which it held that, irrespective of the intent of Congress, the status of share taxation had not been changed in any particular.[66] Hence, the states faced again

[63] *Cong. Record,* 69th Cong., 1st sess., p. 6089.

[64] *Ibid.,* p. 6217.

[65] See Appendix for the text of the statute.

[66] *First National Bank of Guthrie Center* v. *Anderson,* 269 U. S. 341 (1926).

the situation that the Richmond decision had produced. Whether the small group in the House who manipulated its passage was in ignorance of the probable effect of the phraseology concocted by them cannot of course be determined. In any event, the door to endless litigation, tax nullification, and the practice of taxation by gentlemen's agreement was again widely ajar.

CHAPTER V

THE MOVEMENT FOR THE FURTHER
AMENDMENT OF SECTION 5219

THE nullification by the court of the attempt of Congress in 1923 to liberalize the share tax provision of Section 5219 imparted new motivation to the legislative movement to increase the latitude of the states with respect to national bank taxation. On March 21, 1927, the Minnesota,[1] Wisconsin,[2] and Kentucky[3] cases were handed down by the Supreme Court of the United States. In these cases it was established beyond all possible doubt that national bank taxes were voidable in any state where it could be shown that a substantial amount of competing moneyed capital held by corporations or private individuals was either exempt from property taxation or was in fact subject to a lower tax rate than national bank shares.[4] Such moneyed capital *did not have to compete with all the operations* of national banks but only with *some* of those activities. Moreover, the powers of national banks had been broadened, by the passage of the McFadden Act of 1927,[5] to include trust operations, increased real estate loans, savings deposits, and investment transactions. By the same token the area of competition between private investments and such banks was considerably widened.

Meanwhile, the campaign for the amendment of Section 5219, the publicity given by the press to these activities, the interest created by the hearings thereon, the effectiveness of banking associations and banking journals in keeping the bankers of the country constantly informed as to the changing status of bank taxation,

[1] *Minnesota* v. *First National Bank of St. Paul,* 273 U. S. 561 (1927).
[2] *First National Bank of Hartford* v. *Hartford,* 273 U. S. 548 (1927)
[3] *Georgetown National Bank* v. *McFarland,* 273 U. S. 568 (1927).
[4] See chap. 3, *supra.*
[5] *United States Statutes at Large,* XLIV, 1224 ff.

and the rising burden of state and local taxation, sometimes discriminatory against banks, all combined to produce a constantly increasing harvest of bank tax litigation. Banking organizations now flatly refused to countenance the suggestion of further amendment to Section 5219, taking the position that the 1926 Amendment gave the states adequate latitude for the imposition of just taxes on the banks.[6]

Minnesota was the first state to promote aggressively a campaign for further amendment of Section 5219. Following the Minnesota decision, the legislature of that state created the Bank Tax Commission to investigate the bank tax situation, collate information as to the states concerned, formulate the issues involved, and present them to Congress.[7] The National Tax Association, which now refused to go on record in favor of further amendment, took no part as an association in the promotion of the movement, but its sessions in Toronto, October 10-16, 1927, brought together a group of people interested in the issue.[8] Representatives of thirty-three states met and appointed a committee to carry the issue of bank taxation to Congress.[9]

Accordingly, hearings were held on February 2, 24, and 29, 1928, before the Senate Committee on Banking and Currency on a bill, S. 1573, to amend Section 5219 which provided that the limiting measure on the share taxation of national banks should be the rate "assessed upon other moneyed capital used or employed in the business of banking."[10] Subsequently, on May 10-

[6] American Bankers Association Supplement, *Commercial and Financial Chronicle*, 1927, p. 84; *ibid.*, 1928, p. 82; A. B. A. *Journal*, XVIII, 687 ff.; *ibid.*, XIX, 402.

[7] *Laws of 1927*, chap. 382; *Hearings* before Senate Banking and Currency Committee, on S. 1573, 70th Cong., 1st sess. (1928), p. 2.

[8] *Proceedings*, N. T. A., 1927, pp. 317 ff.

[9] Senate *Hearings*, 1928, p. 2.

[10] *Ibid.*, p. 1; introduced by Senator Norbeck and referred to the Committee on Dec. 12, 1927; *Congressional Record*, 70th Cong., 1st sess., p. 476.

11, 1928, hearings were also held by the House Committee on Banking and Currency on H. R. 8727 which proposed to amend Section 5219 by substituting for the other moneyed capital limit on share taxes, "the rate imposed upon the shares of state banks."[11]

At these hearings both the tax authorities and the bankers presented again the arguments which had been advanced in the 1922 hearings, but additional considerations, flowing from the changed situation, were also urged.[12] The tax authorities contended that national bank taxes in twenty-three states were voidable because they exempted moneys and credits, or taxed them at a low rate, and that thirty-three states were involved through the favored tax treatment of real estate mortgages.[13] It was furthermore alleged that the banks were actively contesting the taxes. In Virginia, Minnesota, and Wisconsin,[14] decisions of the United States Supreme Court had already declared national bank share taxes invalid with the result that such taxes as were being paid were collected under a gentlemen's agreement. In Iowa, where money and credits were taxed at a rate of five mills, a case involving certain Des Moines banks seeking a refund of $700,000 was in process.[15] In Polk County, Iowa, five banks were seeking to recover $650,000,[16] and state banks were insisting that they must be taxed as national banks.

Kansas with a low rate on intangibles and a low mortgage

[11] *Hearings* before the House Committee on Banking and Currency, 70th Cong., 1st sess., 1928, p. 1. This bill was introduced by Mr. Goodwin and on Jan. 6, 1928, was referred to the Committee; *Cong. Record.*, 70th Cong., 1st sess., p. 1124.

[12] The Minnesota Commission, meanwhile, had prepared an elaborate brief which showed the status of bank taxation in the several states, and had distributed it to the members of Congress and other interested parties.

[13] Senate *Hearings*, 1928, pp. 15 ff.

[14] Wisconsin, meanwhile, had shifted to income taxation of banks. See chap. 6, *infra*.

[15] Senate *Hearings*, 1928, p. 29.

[16] House *Hearings*, 1928, p. 93.

registry tax was in a similar situation. Suits had been instituted by national banks,[17] and a decision rendered in April, 1928, was in favor of the banks.[18] In Washington, suits by several banks had been pressed on the ground that certain other financial institutions were exempt from taxation.[19] Mortgages and credits were exempt by virtue of a constitutional provision.[20] South Dakota with its four mill tax on moneys and credits was faced with a number of suits and the attorney-general of that state held it would be futile to attempt to tax national banks at a rate in excess of four mills.[21] In Michigan, due to the low rate on mortgages, two national banks had paid their taxes under protest and had started suits.[22] Montana faced trouble by virtue of her scheme of classification and the exemption of mortgages.[23] A number of banks in that state were asking for the cancellation of the last half of 1927 taxes.[24] Though California had reluctantly raised her rate on intangibles to an equality with that on banks, suits were then pending which involved 1926 and 1927 taxes, and all bank taxes were jeopardized by virtue of the exemption of mortgages.[25] In Alabama over a million dollars of bank taxes were involved as moneys and credits were entirely exempt and mortgages were taxed at a low rate. One bank had sued to recover back taxes for a five year period.[26] New Hampshire with its income tax on intangibles was operating on a precarious gentlemen's agreement.[27] In Nebraska several cases were tried in 1926 with

[17] Senate *Hearings,* 1928, pp. 40 ff.
[18] House *Hearings,* 1928, p. 107.
[19] *Ibid.,* pp. 61 f., 118 ff.
[20] Senate *Hearings,* 1928, pp. 27 ff.
[21] *Ibid.,* p. 42.
[22] House *Hearings,* 1928, p. 106; Senate *Hearings,* 1928, p. 23.
[23] Senate *Hearings,* 1928, p. 39.
[24] House *Hearings,* 1928, pp. 67 ff.
[25] *Ibid.,* p. 105; Senate *Hearings,* 1928, pp. 22, 39.
[26] House *Hearings,* 1928, pp. 56 ff.
[27] *Ibid.,* pp. 48 ff.

decisions favorable to the banks.[28] Kentucky was facing a situation not unlike other states as intangibles in that state were taxed at 50 cents while bank stocks were subject to a rate of $1.30 per $100.[29] For these and similar reasons, it was alleged, the tax systems of forty-three states were directly involved.[30] Millions of dollars of taxes were liable to annulment, producing a fiscal situation of momentous consequences to the states.[31]

Vigorous objection was also urged against Section 5219 on the further ground that it coerced the states in the matter of local tax policy. Under it the only alternatives available were (1) the surrender of their schemes of classification and low rate taxation on intangibles, or (2) the taxation of national banks at the lowest rate imposed on any competing intangibles, or (3) the continuance of the policy of taxing banks under gentlemen's agreement. Relative to these alternatives, it was contended that the bankers themselves were opposed to the return to the general property tax and the consequent taxation of moneys, credits, and mortgages at the full property rate.[32] The taxation of intangibles at a low rate was justified both on grounds of expediency and ability to pay, and to return to the old methods would constitute a reversal of the wheels of progress.[33]

To adopt the second alternative and tax bank stock at the lowest rate imposed on intangibles would not be consistent with the demands of justice since banks were going concerns operating with the funds of their depositors and producing large and regular profits considerably in excess of the return reaped by the individual from purely private investments.[34] The loss of revenue

[28] *Ibid.*, p. 107.
[29] *Ibid.*, p. 101.
[30] Senate *Hearings*, 1928, pp. 66 ff.
[31] House *Hearings*, 1928, pp. 56, 64, 93, 105; Senate *Hearings*, 1928, pp. 17, 22, 26, 46.
[32] Senate *Hearings*, 1928, pp. 5, 7, 46.
[33] House *Hearings*, 1928, pp. 98 ff.
[34] Senate *Hearings*, 1928, pp. 44 ff.

from such a change would be great.[85]   Furthermore, it was truthfully asserted that private investments do not come into real and substantial competition with national banks; the alleged competition was only legal and technical, and the taxation of these intangibles at a low rate evinced no hostility to the banks.[36]

Nor was the third alternative within the dignity of the states or the requirements of justice.   Taxation by a gentlemen's agreement was obviously coercive and intolerable.[37]   Nor were adequate revenues obtained.   Furthermore, it was extremely doubtful whether the gentlemen's agreements were legally enforceable.   Indeed some few banks, taking advantage of the letter of the law, refused to abide by them.

The position maintained by the bankers during the hearings was that of uncompromising opposition to further changes in the law.   It was urged that since the 1926 Amendment to Section 5219 the states had abundant latitude in taxing national banks.[38]   The states could employ either the income tax or the excise tax; the latter would permit the states to impose a tax on income from all sources.   Share taxation, it was alleged, was wrong in principle and vicious in practice, as it penalized the bank for building up a large stockholders' equity and thereby imperilled banking safety.[39]   Income taxation, being based on ability to pay, would be fair, in line with progressive trends in taxation, and at the same time yield to the state adequate revenues.[40]   It was claimed that New York, Massachusetts, and Wisconsin had adopted such schemes of bank taxation with satisfactory results.

To these contentions the advocates of further amendment

[85] *Ibid.,* pp. 17 ff.

[36] *Ibid.,* pp. 9, 46.

[37] *Ibid.,* p. 199; House *Hearings,* 1928, p. 48.

[38] House *Hearings,* 1928, pp. 117 ff.

[39] *Ibid.,* pp. 151, 186; Senate *Hearings,* 1928, pp. 106, 117. See chap. 7, *infra.*

[40] House *Hearings,* 1928, pp. 135 ff.

properly replied that not all states could constitutionally employ income taxation, and that the vast majority of state and local revenues were raised by means of ad valorem property taxation. Under such conditions, to tax banks by means of an excise or income tax would result in a lower tax burden on them than was imposed on other subjects.[41] To these objections there may also be added the fiscal inadequacy of such taxation.[42]

The amending bills, however, made no headway. Apparently abandoning the proposal to class banks in a separate group for tax purposes, Senator Norbeck of South Dakota on May 17, 1928, and Mr. Goodwin of Minnesota on May 24, 1928, introduced identical bills into the Senate and the House.[43] These bills, S. 4486 and H. R. 14001, provided that the rate on national bank shares should not be greater than the rate on real estate used for mercantile or like business purposes in the taxing district of the bank, nor higher than the rate assessed on the shares of corporations or individuals engaged in the business of receiving demand deposits in such districts. A further provision would validate such bank taxes previously levied by the states as would be valid under the provisions of the amended bill.[44]

These proposals encountered objections from the banks, an elaborate brief being filed with the House Committee on Banking and Currency in opposition thereto.[45] The comptroller of currency joined the bankers in their efforts to forestall any further amendment[46] as did also Secretary of Treasury, A. W. Mellon.[47] The tax authorities were also active. Memorials to Congress from the state legislatures of Minnesota, Kansas, South Dakota,

[41] *Ibid.,* pp. 69 ff.
[42] See chap. 6, *infra.*
[43] *Congressional Record,* 70th Cong., 1st sess., p. 9793; A. B. A. *Journal,* XXI, 186.
[44] A. B. A. *Journal,* XXI, p. 186.
[45] *Ibid.,* p. 985.
[46] *Report of the Comptroller of Currency,* 1928, pp. 1-3.
[47] *Com. and Fin. Chron.,* CXXVI, 1446.

and Washington calling for relief from the restrictive provisions of Section 5219 were offered.[48] At the meeting of state Governors in November, 1928, Governor Christensen of Minnesota addressed that body on the necessity for amending the federal statute.[49] The issue was also submitted to the Association of Attorney-Generals, and a committee was appointed by that group to consider the problem. A futile effort was made to get a plank in the Republican Platform of 1928 calling for an amendment to Section 5219.[50] Despite this agitation, Congress refused to legislate.

Rebuffed by Congress in their efforts to amend Section 5219, the states sought local remedies. Determined, if possible, not to surrender their schemes of classification and income taxation, nor yet to forego the taxation of banks, they had already proceeded to meet the emergency by changes in their tax laws. New York in June, 1923, passed a law which stipulated that moneyed capital coming into competition with national bank shares should be taxed at the same rate as that imposed on national bank shares, leaving the job of ferreting out such moneys to the tax administrators. By so doing, it was hoped that the income tax on other intangibles, not in competition with banks, could be maintained and the one per cent tax on bank shares legalized. This law was held valid in 1926 by the New York Supreme Court.[51]

Other states took similar action. California in 1927 authorized the taxation of competing moneyed capital at the same rate as that levied on bank stock,[52] as did also Iowa in 1929,[53] Kansas in

[48] A. B. A. *Journal*, XXI, 986; *Congressional Record*, 70th Cong., 2d sess., pp. 3634 ff., 5031.
[49] House *Hearings*, 1930, pp. 145 ff.
[50] A. B. A. *Journal*, XXI, 263.
[51] *People ex el. Pratt* v. *Goldfogle et. al.*, 242 N. Y. 277 (1924).
[52] *Final Report of California Tax Commission*, 1922, pp. 280 ff.
[53] *Revenue Laws of Iowa*, Sec. 7005.

1927,[54] Montana in 1929,[55] North Dakota in 1923,[56] and Virginia in 1928.[57] Vermont in 1925 excluded competing moneyed capital from the provisions of the intangible tax laws.[58] South Dakota in 1923, at the request of the Bankers Association in that state, changed the basis of valuation of bank shares from book value to capital stock alone. It was hoped that this plan would prevent further bank tax litigation, but suits continued in spite of the change.[59] Wyoming pursued a similar policy in 1927.[60] Nebraska placed banks and moneys and credits on the same basis in 1929 the tax rate being fixed at eight mills.[61] In 1927 Oklahoma provided for the taxation of moneys and credits, other than competitive moneyed capital, at a rate of one-fifth of one per cent.[62]

Certain states, however, resorted to the taxation of the income of banks as a solution of the problem. Massachusetts in 1925 experimented with excise taxation. New York[63] and California,[64] after first trying the device of taxing competing moneyed capital at the rate imposed on bank shares, also turned to excise taxation of banks in 1926 and 1929, respectively. Wisconsin in 1926[65] extended its scheme of direct income taxation to banks while Washington[66] and Oregon[67] in 1929 followed California in the adoption of the excise tax alternative.[68] Sub-

[54] *Laws of Kansas,* 1927, chap. 326.
[55] *Laws of 1929, Montana,* H. B. No. 181.
[56] *Laws of 1923,* North Dakota, chap. 307.
[57] *Acts of Assembly* 1928, Virginia, chap. 232.
[58] *Acts of 1925,* Vermont, No. 21.
[59] *Report of the Department of Finance,* South Dakota, 1928, pp. 159 ff.
[60] *Session Laws of 1927,* Wyoming, chap. 75.
[61] *Laws of 1929,* Nebraska, chap. 168.
[62] *Session Laws,* Oklahoma, 1927, chap. 92.
[63] *Laws of 1926,* New York, chap. 286.
[64] *Statutes of 1929,* California, chap. 13.
[65] *Laws of 1927,* Wisconsin, chap. 496.
[66] *Laws of 1929,* Washington, chap. 151.
[67] *Laws Relating to Assessment and Taxation,* Oregon, pp. 93 ff.
[68] See chap. 6, *infra,* for fiscal effects of these changes.

sequently, Alabama, Idaho, Oklahoma, and Utah encountered difficulties with the share tax and shifted to excise taxation.

This growing volume of bank tax legislation served to acquaint an increasing number of states with the character of the situation produced by Section 5219. A large number of states had been apathetic all the while to the movement to amend this statute, either relying on the bankers not to prosecute the advantage which was obviously theirs, or the tax authorities continued in ignorance of the significance of the issues involved. In some states both the tax authorities and the bankers, who initially thought they were not affected, later found that they were directly involved.

Meanwhile, the courts were being appealed to by an increasing number of banks seeking to reduce or nullify their taxes. A further complication was added by the decision of the United States Supreme Court in 1929 holding the Massachusetts law, which attempted to reach income from all sources by means of an excise tax, void as to the income from tax exempt securities.[69] Since excise taxation of banks had been devised with the avowed intention of reaching net income from tax exempt sources, this decision for the moment clearly imperilled all such taxation. In later decisions, however, the court sustained the excise tax laws of New York[70] and California[71] with respect to the inclusion of income from tax exempt sources.

Cases in both federal and state courts continue to whittle down the basis for the share taxation of banks. The Washington bank tax law was nullified in a decision which showed competition from tax favored building and loan associations, trust companies, mutual savings banks, finance companies, industrial loan companies, bond dealers, investment bankers and mortgage loan com-

[69] *McCallen* v. *Commonwealth of Massachusetts,* 279 U. S. 620 (1929).

[70] *Educational Films Corporation* v. *Ward,* 282 U. S. 379 (1931).

[71] *Pacific Co. Limited* v. *Johnson State Treasurer of California,* 279 U. S. 480 (1932). See chap. 6, *infra,* for a discussion of these cases.

panies.[72]   The Oregon law had met a similar fate because real estate mortgages and highway bonds were exempt by law, while other bonds and the shares of finance companies were exempt in practice.[73]   Due to competition from firms and individuals dealing in real estate mortgages, bonds, notes, cattle loan and automobile paper, the maximum rate which could be levied on national banks[74] in Oklahoma was limited to the two mill rate levied on certain intangibles.   By virtue of this situation Oklahoma was forced to adopt the income tax method in 1931.[75]   The Montana classification law was also declared to be in contravention of Section 5219 to the extent that national bank stock was taxed in excess of the rate on intangibles.[76]   Kansas was prevented from taxing national banks at a higher rate than that imposed on mortgages,[77] and state banks were accorded similar rights.[78]   The Idaho bank tax law was also declared to be violative of Section 5219 because of the legal exemption of real estate paper and because stocks and bonds in practice were exempt.[79]   In Florida a bank tax was annulled, not because the competing moneyed capital was legally exempt, but because the assessing officers had intentionally failed to assess it.[80]   The Michigan bank tax law of 1929 was also declared invalid on the ground that it did not permit the deduction of credits secured by mortgages on real property from bank shares, which credits are exempt if the specific registration tax of one-half of one per cent is paid.[81]

[72] *National Bank of Commerce* v. *King Co.,* 280 P. 16 (1929).

[73] *Brotherhood Coöperative National Bank* v. *Hurlburt,* 26 Fed. 957 (1928).

[74] *Bonaparte* v. *American First National Bank,* 281 P. 958 (1929).

[75] *Session Laws of Oklahoma,* 1931, chap. 66, Art. 7; *Board of County Commissioners* v. *State Board of Equalization,* 8 P. (2d) 732 (1932).

[76] *State ex. rel Conrad Banking Corporation* v. *Mady,* 272 P. 69 (1928).

[77] *Central National Bank* v. *McFarland,* 20 Fed. (2d) 416 (1927).

[78] *Voran* v. *Wright,* 284 P. 807 (1930).

[79] *Boise City National Bank* v. *Ada County,* 37 Fed. 947 (1930).

[80] *Roberts* v. *American National Bank,* 121 Southern 554 (1929).

[81] *First National Bank of Wyandottee et al.* v. *Common Council of Detroit,* 234 N. W. 151 (1931).

In the face of the increasing nullification of share taxes, the banks for a while vigorously refused to countenance an amendment to Section 5219, contending that the states could resort to income and excise taxation of banks. When, however, the McCallen Case temporarily raised doubts as to the validity of the excise tax on income from tax exempt securities, they relaxed their opposition. Perhaps, too, some bankers were growing restive under the charge that they were using the federal statute as a shield to evade state taxation. In any event, negotiations between tax officials and the bankers were resumed and in 1930 a complex compromise bill was drawn up which proposed to relate the share tax on banks to the tax burden on other corporations, using income as a measure of the tax load. The bill also sought to circumvent the effect of the McCallen decision by a cleverly devised fifth alternative. Certain state representatives, notably those from Minnesota, Massachusetts, and New York were disposed to accept the measure, but vigorous opposition arose from the tax officials of a number of states.[82] Objections were voiced to the employment of the income comparatives as unworkable, too complex, and productive of litigation. Corporations by whose tax burdens the levies on banks were to be measured began strenuously to object to being drawn into the bank tax embroglio. A much simpler method of taxing banks was demanded by the states.

As opposition to this bill developed, other proposals were presented. Senator Norbeck of South Dakota introduced a bill, S. 1550, on February 27, 1931, in the third session of the Seventy-first Congress which proposed as the limit on the share tax the rate on moneyed capital employed in the business of banking. This proposal was favorably reported by the Banking and Currency Committee of the Senate but made no further progress.[83]

[82] See State Taxation of National Banks, *Hearings* before House Committee on Banking and Currency on H. R. 7752, 71st Cong., 2d sess.

[83] *Congressional Record,* 71st Cong., 3rd sess., pp. 6232, 6964.

Efforts to amend Section 5219 in the Seventy-second Congress also proved futile. Senator Norbeck again presented his proposal, S. 4291, on April 1, 1932, but it succeeded only in obtaining a favorable report from the committee.[84] Two bills introduced in the House, H. R. 7928 by Mr. Goodwin on January 18, 1932, and H. R. 11118 by Mr. Steagall on April 5, 1932, were interred in the appropriate committee as was also a second proposal, S. 4986, introduced by Senator Norbeck in the concluding days of the session in July, 1932.[85] The Senate committee also conducted hearings at which time representatives from California, among others, urged their dissatisfaction with the operation of the excise tax on banks and pleaded with the committee to change the federal law so as to permit the states to tax national banks on a basis of equality with other enterprises.[86]

Nor did the first session of the Seventy-third Congress produce any results. Senator Norbeck again offered his proposal, S. 1502 on April 21, 1933 which was duly referred to the appropriate committee.[87] At this session, Representative Hancock of North Carolina introduced a measure, H. R. 5045, on April 17, 1933, which proposed as the limit on share taxation "the moneyed capital used or employed in business and coming into substantial competition with the business of national banks in normal banking activities."[88] It also made no progress beyond reference to the committee.

In the second session a bill, S. 2788, introduced by Senator Fletcher of Florida on February 15, 1934, was favorably reported by the Banking and Currency Committee.[89] It proposed no basic change from the present share tax provision but did extend the

[84] *Ibid.,* 72d Cong., 1st sess., pp. 7251, 9299.
[85] *Ibid.,* pp. 2205, 7520, 15698.
[86] *Hearings,* on S. 4291, 72d Cong., 1st sess.
[87] *Congressional Record,* 73d Cong., 1st sess., p. 2064.
[88] *Ibid.,* p. 1859.
[89] *Ibid.,* 2d sess., pp. 2543, 4227, 4879, 5727.

protective features of Section 5219 to such state banks and trust companies as were members of the Federal Reserve System. Another proposal in the Senate, S. 3009, introduced by Senator Shipstead of Minnesota, on March 9, 1934, would provide for such state taxation of national banks on income and/or property as was imposed on state banks.[90] It never advanced beyond the committee. A similar measure in the House, H. R. 9045, introduced on April 10, 1934, by Representative Steagall of Alabama was reported with some amendments from the House Committee but never passed that body.[91] The two last mentioned bills were favored by the tax officials but were vigorously opposed by the banks.[92] Hearings on the proposals to amend were conducted by the House Committee, at which time little additional information was presented. The need for action was again urged by the representatives from the states as national banks were not paying adequate taxes. It was asserted that the states had lost $250,000,-000 of taxes in the last seven years due to the failure to amend Section 5219.[93]

And thus the situation remains. With share taxes on national banks either void or voidable in every state in which it can be shown that competing moneyed capital is taxed, if at all, at a lower rate than that in fact imposed on such shares, Congress has for eight years failed to act. Though in a few recent decisions there seems to be a tendency on the part of the court to require more conclusive proof of a violation of Section 5219, there is not a single state employing the share tax method in which substantial legal grounds do not exist for its invalidation.

[90] *Ibid.*, p. 4041.
[91] *Ibid.*, pp. 6375, 10294.
[92] Saxe, "Section 5219 in the Seventy-third Congress," A. B. A. *Journal,* May, 1934, p. 33.
[93] *Hearings* on H. R. 9045, 73d Cong., 2d sess., p. 32.

CHAPTER VI

INCOME AND EXCISE TAXATION OF BANKS

WISCONSIN was the first state to employ the direct income tax alternative provided by Section 5219. Soon after the Richmond decision the validity of the Wisconsin share tax provision was challenged and finally invalidated in 1927.[1] Meanwhile, the taxes on bank shares were compromised on a basis of 50 per cent for the years, 1921-1924, and on an income tax basis for 1925 and 1926. In 1927 the income tax law applicable to non-banking corporations was amended to include banks.[2] The rates now applicable to banks are graduated as follows: 2 per cent on the first $1000 of taxable income; 2½ per cent on the second; 3 per cent on the third; 3½ per cent on the fourth; 4 per cent on the fifth; 5 per cent on the sixth; and 6 per cent on the seventh thousand and on all income in excess of that amount. In addition to these normal rates, a surtax on all taxable income in excess of $3000 equal in amount to one-sixth of the normal tax was imposed in 1931.[3]

Oklahoma also adopted an income tax on banks and business corporations in 1931,[4] but in 1933 changed the tax on national and state banks to a privilege tax according to or measured by net income.[5] Instrumental in the change from share taxation was the fact that the maximum rate which could be imposed on such shares was twenty cents on each $1000 of taxable value. Idaho in 1931 also enacted an income tax law apparently applicable to banks but did not repeal the share tax, whereupon the attorney-general ruled that national banks were not subject to its pro-

[1] *First National Bank of Hartford* v. *Hartford*, 273 U. S. 548 (1927).
[2] *Laws of Wisconsin*, 1927, chap. 396.
[3] *Wisconsin Statutes*, 1931, chap. 71, sec. 71.10, 71.26.
[4] *Session Laws of Oklahoma*, 1931, chap. 66, Art. 7.
[5] *Ibid.*, 1933, chap. 191.

visions.[6] In 1933 the legislature adopted the franchise tax on banks.[7] Wisconsin remains, therefore, the only state which has amply tested the income tax on banks. It has not proved very productive, yielding only $405,720 in 1928, and $453,920, before office audit corrections, in 1929.[8] These amounts were 20.5 per cent and 26.6 per cent of the share taxes imposed in 1926; hence the income tax is yielding about one-fifth the tax it supplanted.

Other patent objections are urged against the direct income tax on banks. Income from tax exempt securities owned by the bank is not taxable. This has reduced considerably the yield in Wisconsin as the exempt income in 1929 was 27 per cent of the taxable income of banks for that year. Furthermore, it results in a significant discrimination as between state and national banks as the ratio of the income from tax exempt bonds to total taxable income of national banks was 37.5 per cent, as against 19.2 per cent for state banks.[9] A marked tax advantage therefore accrues to national banks due to their larger holdings of tax exempt securities.

Nor can this method of taxation be said to be just, when measured by ability to pay, since a dollar earned from tax exempt sources possesses equal tax capacity with the dollar earned from taxable sources. The fact that the *gross income* from tax exempt bonds is not charged with any of the operating expenses of the bank further reduces the net taxable income.[10] The bankers

[6] *Idaho Extraordinary Session*, 1931, chap. 2; *The Tax Digest*, 1932, p. 302.

[7] *Idaho Session Laws*, 1933, chap. 159.

[8] Letter from Chairman Kelly of the Tax Commission.

[9] *Report of Wisconsin Tax Commission*, 1930, pp. 40 ff.

[10] While the court has not passed directly on this issue, the practice is to exempt from taxation the gross income from tax exempt securities. In *Missouri* v. *Gehner*, 281 U. S. 313 (1930), it was held that in the taxation of the net assets of a taxpayer the state could not apportion the liabilities of the taxpayer between taxable and non-taxable assets but had to allow the full deduction of the liabilities against the taxable assets for purposes of taxing net worth. See also R. J. Traynor, "Taxation Problems in Branch Banking," *Minnesota Law Review*, XV, 778 ff.

themselves recognized the injustices involved in the taxation of income and supported the movement for excise taxation. For these and other reasons[11] only Wisconsin employs this method and the emergency conditions existing in that state at the time of its adoption unquestionably were influential in its selection.

Section 5219 also extends to the states the privilege of taxing as personal income the dividends paid on national bank shares to the shareholder. Such taxes are not in fact imposed on the banks, and but one state has adopted this exclusive alternative. Vermont in 1931 authorized the inclusion of bank dividends in the taxable investment income of individuals subject to the rate of 4 per cent.[12] National banks are directly taxable in that state only on their real property. It need only be added that this method is the least productive alternative which a state may select.

Excise[13] taxation of banks had its initiation in Massachusetts in the effort to reach the income from tax exempt securities.[14] As a corporate privilege tax, it was hoped that values could be included in the measure of the tax which were not themselves directly taxable. With the actual or threatened invalidation of share taxes, Massachusetts, New York, California, Utah, Washington, Oregon, Oklahoma, Idaho, and Alabama adopted the excise or franchise tax. The chief provisions of the excise tax laws of these states are summarized in Table I below. The Washington, Oregon, and Utah laws differ from those of the eastern states by permitting certain real estate and/or personal property tax off-

[11] The objections applying to excise taxation, in part, apply likewise to the direct income tax. See *infra*.

[12] *Laws of Vermont,* 1931, No. 17, sec. 4.

[13] The terms "Excise" and "Franchise" are used interchangeably to denote a tax on the corporate privilege.

[14] The Massachusetts law ran afoul of the court in its effort to tax indirectly the income from tax exempt securities but the California statute, with a change in the personnel of the court, hurdled this difficulty. See *Educational Films Corporation* v. *Ward,* 282 U. S. 379 (1931); *Pacific Company* v. *Johnson,* 285 U. S. 480 (1932).

sets. Massachusetts and California present a further variation by leaving the determination of the rate to the tax commissioner, subject to a maximum of 6 per cent, whereas the rates imposed by the other states are prescribed by the statute. In all cases the states attempted to comply with the terms of the binding federal statute in that the rate on banks must not be higher than "the highest rate assessed upon other financial corporations nor higher than the highest of the rates assessed by the taxing state upon mercantile, manufacturing, and business corporations."

Despite the aggressive sponsorship of the franchise tax by the bankers, its acceptance has not as yet been generally achieved. Unquestionably, the chief reason for the reluctance of the states to adopt it, even in the face of the voidability of their share taxes, is the loss of revenue which such change would entail. So far the excise tax on banks has not possessed the virtue of fiscal adequacy. While the data as to the yield of such taxes are limited, such as are available indicate clearly that the revenue derived from this method of bank taxation is much less than that derived from the preceding share taxes.

In Massachusetts the excise tax during the first five years of its operation produced on the average only 36 per cent of the average share tax during the three years preceding its invalidation. Measured in terms of the percentage of income before taxes, the ratio varies from 3.36 per cent in 1928 to 6.68 per cent in 1930, and in terms of a property tax equivalent on book value the range is between 2.7 and 3.8 mills.

The franchise tax on banks in New York for the four years, 1927-1930, varied from 2.88 per cent of income before taxes in 1927 to 4.37 per cent in 1930.[15] When reduced to a property tax equivalent, the franchise tax was slightly more than a three mill levy on book value.

[15] Computed from reports of the Tax Commission and Comptroller of Currency. Income before taxes as here used is net profits plus taxes as reported to the comptroller.

STATE TAXATION OF BANKS

The fiscal results of the franchise tax on banks in California have also proved disappointing. In its first three years, 1929-

TABLE I. THE EXCISE TAX ON BANKS

STATE— Legal Citation	Measure of Tax	Rate	Assessment Collection	Distribution
ALABAMA Gen. Acts of Ala. 1933, Act 111.	Net income from all sources	5%	State Tax Commission	After expenses, ¼ to state, ¼ to towns, ½ to county.
CALIFORNIA Cal. Stat. 1929, ch. 13. Cal Stat. 1931, ch. 65. Cal. Stat. 1933, ch. 303.	Net income from all sources	Fixed by Com'r; maximum 6%	Tax Com'r	General fund of state
IDAHO Session Laws 1933, ch. 159.	Net income from all sources	1% on first $1000 2% on second $1000 3% on third $1000 4% on fourth $1000 5% on fifth $1000 6% on excess	Tax Com'r	General fund to reduce property tax.
MASSACHUSETTS Gen. Law, ch. 63 as amended by Acts of 1930, ch. 220, Acts of 1933, ch. 327.	Net income from all sources	Fixed by Com'r; maximum 6%	Tax Com'r	Pro-rata to stockholders. Residents to town. Non-residents to state.
NEW YORK Con. Laws, 1930, ch. 61, s. 219 p.	Net income from all sources	4½%	Tax Com'r	Localities, pro-rata assessed property.
OKLAHOMA Session Laws 1933 ch. 195.	Net income from all sources except tax-free U.S. securities	1% on first $2000 2% on next $2000 3% on next $3000 4% on next $3000 5% on next $4000 6% on remainder	Tax Com'r	¼ to state, ¾ to public school after 5% for collection and refunds.
OREGON Oregon Laws 1929, ch. 427. Oregon Laws 1931, ch. 273.	Net income from all sources	8%	Tax Com'r	General funds of state.
UTAH Laws of Utah, 1931, ch. 39.	Net income from all taxable sources	3%	Tax Com'r	¾ to district school fund, ¼ to general fund of state.
*WASHINGTON Laws of 1929, ch. 151.	Net income from all sources	5% offset of tangible personal property	Tax Com'r	State and counties pro-rata to state and local rates.

*Declared invalid by State Supreme Court. *Barr* v. *Chase* 289, P. 551 (1930); *Aberdeen Savings and Loan Association* v. *Chase* 289 P. 536 (1930).

1931, it produced $2,292,225 as compared with a yield of $13,-499,374 during the last three years of the 1.45 per cent rate on bank shares.[16] The revenue derived was but 17 per cent of the prior share tax. In 1929 and 1930, respectively, the franchise tax was only 1.37 and 1.80 mills of the book value of bank shares. The lower yield in California, as compared with New York and Massachusetts, is due to the then lower tax rate and the offset of 10 per cent of the real estate tax, if not in excess of 75 per cent of the excise tax. Changes in the law in 1933 which eliminated the offset and raised the maximum rate to 6 per cent should appreciably increase the productivity of the tax.[17]

The excise tax of 5 per cent in Oregon in 1930 produced $124,736 from banks, or 19 per cent of the preceding share tax yield of $653,000.[18] A share tax of 3.4 mills on book value would have returned as much as the excise tax. Dissatisfied with the returns the rate was raised to 8 per cent in 1931 which, it was estimated, would produce $199,189.[19]

In view of these data, it would appear that the charge of fiscal inadequacy has a real basis. The solution might be suggested by the action of Oregon in raising the rate. Such a course is feasible if all revenues are obtained by taxes on or measured by income. In point of fact, however, this condition does not obtain. Every state imposes property taxation, which is independent of income, and many states also add multiple levies such as license, sales, excises on commodities and privilege taxes. In a majority of states employing the income tax, or the franchise tax measured by income, it is in the nature of a supplementary levy rather than

[16] *Summary Report of the California Tax Research Bureau*, 1932, p. 75.

[17] Deering, *Codes, Laws and Constitutional Amendments of California*, 1933 Supplement, Act 8488; Traynor and Keesling, "Recent Changes in Bank and Corporation Franchise Tax Act," *California Law Review*, XXI, 543-56.

[18] Eleventh *Biennial Report of Tax Commission*, Oregon, pp. 15 ff.

[19] *Ibid.*, p. 17; *Oregon Laws*, 1931, chap. 273.

an exclusive method of taxation. Therefore it is apparent that to tax banks equally with other subjects necessitates a higher rate of excise taxation than the state can apply to other corporations which are subject to multiple forms of taxation. Here lies a major objection to the fourth alternative offered by Section 5219.

It has been contended that Section 5219 now permits the equalization of bank taxes with all business taxes, exclusive of taxes on real estate, imposed on those corporations by whose burden the bank tax is measured. It is said that the states may follow the example of Massachusetts and California in leaving the determination of the rate to be applied to banks to the tax administrators who will employ the yard stick of taxes to net income in arriving at such a rate.[20]

The validity of this procedure, however, has not been established by the courts. Furthermore, it is obvious that before the rate on banks can be determined elaborate statistical analyses of the tax burden on other corporations must be made, unless such corporations are subjected to the same type and rate of taxation as is applied to banks.[21] The determination of the bases for such taxation is by no means simple. In arriving at the tax burden on other corporations both net income and the total state and local taxes must be obtained. To secure accurate income data is very difficult. In the first place, net income is itself subject to multiple definition. Mr. Blodgett of Connecticut cites five definitions of net income, all differing in important respects.[22] The courts might conceivably take any one of these definitions, and the tax administrator another. Net income, too, is largely a function of the peculiarities of the accounting system and may easily be increased or diminished by adjusting depreciation, obsolescence,

[20] Nichols, "State Taxation of National Banks," A. B. A. sup., *Com. and Fin. Chron.*, 1928, pp. 84 ff.; Saxe, "The Threatened Discrimination in Banking Taxation," *Bankers Magazine*, CV, 785 ff.

[21] *Report of Minnesota Tax Commission*, 1928, p. 152.

[22] Blodgett, N. T. A., *Bul.*, XVI, 74.

depletion, and other charges which are inevitably approximations.

Effective excise tax administration also requires elaborate machinery to define and enforce the thousands of rules necessary to secure standard returns; the auditing of these returns must be carefully and expertly done, and even then, tax refunds are large and delayed auditing quite frequent. Difficult questions as to the treatment of group losses are raised, on which as yet no judicial interpretations have been given. Finally, comparisons are impossible when no net income for a group exists; in such instances the income comparative breaks down completely.

As to the taxes which are to be used as the numerator of the ratio, it is urged that the records available are incomplete, inaccurate, and unreliable. Knotty questions arise as to the exclusion or inclusion of organization fees, motor vehicle taxes, gasoline taxes and licenses in the measure. Furthermore, some corporations report taxes on a cash basis while others employ an accrual method.[23]

There are different kinds of averages, and quite different results are obtained from the use of a simple arithmetical average, a mode, or median in the measurement of the rate as between banks and financial, mercantile, manufacturing, and other business corporations. In summary, the computation of relative tax burden as between banks and the corporations by whose rate the bank tax is to be limited is far from the simple procedure pictured by its advocates.[24] It would involve, instead, extensive statistical analyses and administrative expense which is not compensated by the small income to be derived from the banks by the use of this method.

Objection to franchise taxation is also urged on the ground that the federal law is cumbersome, complex and ambiguous. The corporations by whose burden the rate on bank income is limited

[23] *Ibid.*, p. 77.
[24] House *Hearings*, 1930, p. 157.

have not been judicially defined. Does the term "financial corporations," for instance, include or exclude insurance companies, building and loan associations, and savings banks? Mercantile, manufacturing, and other business corporations have not been judicially determined for purposes of this act. It is not clear into which group certain corporations will fall, since many companies have very broad charter rights and do not readily conform to prescribed legal categories. The area of litigation opened up by this alternative appears to be quite large, particularly when the judicial evolution of Section 5219 is recalled.

Significant of the judicial hurdles such a complicated income comparative tax on banks faces are the decisions so far rendered. The Massachusetts law was declared invalid as to income from tax exempt securities.[25] The New York statute was held valid in this respect[26] as was also the California statute[27] following a change in the personnel of the court. All of these cases involved a non-banking corporation. The Washington statute ran afoul the state court, however, because the tax classification which included only banks and financial institutions, and did not include partnerships and individuals doing a similar business, was held too narrow and arbitrary to be valid.[28] As a result the only tax imposed in 1932 on banks in Washington was the levy on real property.[29]

Presumably, therefore, a franchise tax on corporations must include a sufficiently large variety of enterprises to establish its standing as a privilege tax. Proponents of the excise tax have contended that the states could employ this method of taxing banks without being compelled to readjust their corporate tax-

[25] *McCallen* v. *Commonwealth of Massachusetts,* 279 U. S. 620 (1929).
[26] *Educational Films Corporation* v. *Ward,* 282 U. S. 388 (1931).
[27] *Pacific Company Limited* v. *Johnson,* 285 U. S. 480 (1932).
[28] *Barr* v. *Chase,* 289 P. 551 (1930) ; *Aberdeen Saving and Loan Association* v. *Chase,* 289 P. 536 (1930).
[29] Fourth *Biennial Report of Tax Commission,* 1932, p. 18.

ation in other respects.[30]   In this they were possibly in error.   The constitutional use of franchise taxation of banks would seem to require a more or less comprehensive reorganization of the plan of corporate taxation in those states which do not already use franchise taxation in the manner contemplated by Section 5219. Since a large number of states employ corporate franchise taxation as a more or less nominal capital stock tax and rely for revenue primarily on the taxation of the property and corporate excess of such companies, thorough-going readjustments in the tax structures of such states may possibly be necessary to validate the excise tax on national banks.   Again the coercive character of Section 5219 is apparent.

It should also be noted with respect to the franchise taxation of national banks that its constitutionality may be questioned on other grounds.   Prior to the 1926 Amendment to Section 5219, the court had held the taxation of the franchise of a national bank invalid.[31]   If such taxation is now sustained by the court, it must be based on the theory that Congress has the power to waive the immunity of national banks as federal agencies from direct taxation by the states.   There is also the unsolved issue as to whether such legislation will conflict with the due process and equal protection clause of the Constitution, particularly in those states where offsets are permitted to other corporations and are not extended to national banks.

Excise taxation is subject to attack on grounds of theory.   The depression had conclusively shown that tax systems cannot be constructed solely on the basis of income.   Property is as essential in the construction of a tax system as is income.[32]   Banks earning no net income require and receive the protective services offered by the government just as truly as do banks whose income ac-

[30] See chap. 5, *supra.*
[31] *Owensboro National Bank* v. *Owensboro,* 173 U. S. 664 (1899).
[32] Leland, *op. cit.,* pp. 408 ff.

counts reflect a profit. Taxes are as much a fixed charge on society and its component institutions as are private rents, interest, or wages. The highly fluctuating character of corporate and personal income makes the status of governmental revenues exceedingly precarious if they rest alone on the income base. Fiscal necessity requires some type of stable taxation. The rapid adoption of sales taxation in recent years supports this contention. Therefore, to apply to banks, alone, the test of income, while other tax subjects are being taxed on property, sales, franchise, and/or income, is discriminatory and violative of recognized principles of sound finance.

The actual operation of the excise tax, so far, has failed to justify the claims which its proponents have advanced. Proposed as an equitable solution of the bank tax problem for the states facing the invalidation of share taxes by virtue of the low millage rates on intangibles, it has failed to produce as much revenue as the usual three, four, or five mill rates on the invested capital of banks would have produced. Any advantages that inhere in its use accrue to the banks in substantially reduced taxes. It had also been urged that the excise method by imposing a tax on income from all sources would operate to produce equality of taxation as between banks and other corporations. But the inclusion of income from tax exempt sources was invalidated by the courts in Massachusetts and Washington. Hence this tax cannot be said to have achieved that nominal equality in effective rate which was expected. More important still is the fact that in most states other corporations are called upon to bear additional types of taxation which cannot now be imposed on banks. To tax banks on their income while other corporations are subject to multiple taxation is to favor banks.

CHAPTER VII

THE TAXATION OF BANK SHARES AT GENERAL
PROPERTY RATES

PRIOR to the establishment of the National Banking System,
banks were taxed in different ways by the several states.
Taxes on income, capital, shares, and dividends were employed,
and a number of states resorted to combinations of income and
property taxes sometimes at high rates. Since the tax clause of
the National Bank Act of 1864 permitted the states to tax only
the shares and real property of national banks, the taxation of
share capital either at a uniform rate or at general property rates
became universal for national banks. Despite the amendments to
Section 5219 authorizing income and excise taxation, share taxation still remains the most widely employed method. Twenty-
two states tax banks at general property rates and fifteen use the
uniform rate.

The chief provisions of the laws of the general property tax
states are summarized in Table II. It is open to question whether
South Dakota and Kansas should be included in this group since
court decisions have invalidated the general property rate on bank
shares in those states. Since the state statutes still provide for
such share taxation these states have been so classified.

Prior to 1931 banks did not issue preferred stock or capital
notes. In the effort to strengthen their capital structure, a large
number of them have since sold preferred stock to the Recon-
struction Finance Corporation and other parties. The state taxable status of such issues is a matter of some uncertainty. Section
5219 hardly contemplated preferred issues though conceivably the
term "shares" could be interpreted to include preferred as well as
common stock. In contemplation such preferred stock issues represent temporary and emergency financing and could very prop-

[91]

Table II. The General Property Tax States

State—Legal Citation	Basis of Assessment	Deductions
Arizona Rev. Code 1928, Ch. 75, s. 3068-74	Full cash value	Book value of real estate
Arkansas C. &. M. Digest, 1921, Ch. 168, s. 9945-52	Market value	Assessed value of real estate

Colorado
Comp. Laws, 1921,
  Ch. 155, s. 7450-53
	Market value with
	  book value as a guide
		Assessed value of real estate

Georgia Georgia Code, 1933, s. 92-406	Market value	Assessed value of real estate
Illinois Tax Laws, 1933, pp. 76-78	Market value	Assessed value of real estate
Kansas 1931 Sup. to R.S. 1923, s. 79-1101	True value	Assessed value of real estate

Louisiana
Dart. Gen. Stat. 1932,
  Ch. 8, s. 684-89
	Book value	Book value of real estate
		Equity in building company own-
		  ing bank premises

Michigan
Pub. Acts, 1931, Act 94
	Cash value	Assessed value of real estate
		Investment in building company
		Exempt securities in proportion
		  of book value to book value
		  and deposits

Minnesota
Laws of 1925, Ch. 304
Laws of 1931, Ch. 303
Laws of 1933, Ch. 315
	⅓ of actual value
	  (Taxes compromised
	  on 75% basis)
		Investment in legally owned real
		  estate

Missouri Laws of 1931, H.B. 507	Cash value	Value of real estate
Mississippi Code of 1930, s. 3125, 3138-40	Book Value	True value of real estate
Montana Laws of 1929, Ch. 64	30% of full value	Assessed value of real estate

Nevada
Comp. Laws, 1929,
  s. 6571-77
	Cash value	Proportionate value of real estate;
		  mortgages on which the bank
		  has paid the tax

STATE—Legal Citation	Basis of Assessment	Deductions
NEW MEXICO Stat. of 1929, s. 141-502, 504	Capital plus surplus, in excess of 50% of capital, and undivided profits	Assessed value of legally owned real estate
NORTH CAROLINA Code of 1931, s. 7971	Actual value with book value as a guide	Assessed value of real property; U.S. & N.C. bonds and uncollectibles up to 5% of receivables deductible from surplus and undivided profits
NORTH DAKOTA Laws of 1931, Ch. 294	Book value	Net investment in real estate and taxed personal property
SOUTH CAROLINA Code of 1932, s. 2578, 2663-77	True value	Book value of real estate; U.S. and S.C. bonds and bonds of F.F.L. Bank of Columbia up to 25% of capital and surplus
SOUTH DAKOTA Comp. Laws, 1929, s. 6696-98	Book value subject to true value	Investment in real estate; Surplus and undivided profits taxed at 4 mill rate
TENNESSEE Code of 1932, s. 1391-1403	Cash value	Assessed value of real estate and personal property
TEXAS Rev. Civ. Stat. 1925 Ch. 6, Art. 7165-66	True value	Assessed value of real estate
WEST VIRGINIA Code of 1931, Ch. 11, s. 672	True value	Assessed value of real estate or equity in bank building; debts of shareholders if filed
WYOMING Sess. Laws, 1931, Ch. 122	Par value	Assessed value of real estate

erly be exempted from state taxation on grounds of public policy. Wyoming,[1] New Hampshire,[2] and Vermont[3] have explicitly exempted these issues.

[1] *Session Laws of Wyoming*, 1933, chap. 8.
[2] *New Hampshire Laws*, 1933, chap. 115.
[3] *Laws of Vermont*, 1933, No. 121.

The share tax, though assessed nominally to the stockholder, is generally paid and absorbed by the bank. In legal fiction the bank is the agent of the shareholder authorized to pay the tax. The bank is given a lien on the dividends, or shares, or both until properly reimbursed for the tax. Recognition of the fact that it is a tax on the bank was extended in the permission granted the banks to deduct, as an expense, such share taxes for federal income tax purposes.[4]

The taxation of bank shares at general property rates is but one application of general property taxation. The theoretical defects of the general property tax have been clearly elucidated.[5] Its implicit assumption that property is homogeneous, its adoption of a dubious test of faculty, its failure to consider income as a standard of capacity to pay, and its disregard of tax incidence qualify the theoretical adequacy of this type of taxation. The numerous operative defects which express themselves in discriminations between persons, types of property, tax districts, and properties of differing values are also well known.

In its application to bank shares these defects are plainly visible. The taxation of bank shares at full property rates tends to take a large percentage of the net income of banks.[6] The inherent differences between bank shares and other types of property account for many of the anomalies in bank taxation. Likewise, its operative defects work with particular severity on banks. With assessment and collection at the source, bank shares tend to be assessed at a much higher percentage of full value than other property, thereby discriminations against banks result. Efforts of several states to ameliorate these discriminations through various deductions from the assessment base have multiplied the discriminations as among banks while modifying the discriminations as between banks and other property.[7]

[4] *U. S. Statutes at Large*, XLII, chap. 136.   [6] See *infra*.
[5] Leland, *op. cit.*, chap. 1.   [7] See *infra*.

A satisfactory evaluation of the taxation of bank shares at general property rates necessitates a minute examination of its detailed operation. The problems arising out of the practices of the several states with respect to the *situs* of assessment, the assessment base with the deductions allowed therefrom, and the agencies of assessment require analysis.

With respect to the *situs* of assessment, Section 5219 requires the assessment of the shares held by non-residents at the location of the bank. Most states tax all shares at the *situs* of the bank, but Colorado, Michigan, and Texas do not pursue this practice with respect to shares held by residents. Logical considerations favor the rule of business *situs*. This practice insures the uniform taxation of all the shares of the same bank. When shares held by residents follow the rule of personal *situs* and the shares of non-residents are taxed at the location of the bank, substantial differences in the effective rates on the shares of the same institution may result, both because the tax rates and the ratios of assessment vary in the several taxing districts.

Administrative convenience, uniform and effective assessment, and equality of tax treatment as among shareholders of the same bank point to the desirability of the rule of business *situs* in assessing bank shares. Evasion, discrimination, and conspiracy sometimes follow the practice of personal *situs*.[8] Since the tax is in reality a tax on the bank, there appears to be no justification for the rule of personal *situs*.

The basis of the assessment of bank shares also varies. The laws of most states require the assessment of property at "true cash value," "market value," "actual value," or some other synonym of market value. New Mexico, North Dakota, and South Dakota require the assessment on book value, while Col-

[8] For instances in point, see *Report of Board of State Tax Commissioners*, Michigan, 1902, p. 94; *Report of Maine Tax Commission*, 1908, pp. 55 ff.

orado, Minnesota, and North Carolina stipulate that book value shall be used as a guide in the determination of market value. Wyoming employs par value as the assessment base.

The use of market value is justified on the ground that it possesses most fully the attribute of reality in that it reflects good will and expert management which may or may not be expressed in book value. Theoretically, market value is the proper basis of assessment, but there are practical difficulties in its use. It is often unavailable because of the infrequency of sales.[9] Market value is also subject to wide fluctuations, and the price on the day of assessment may not be truly representative.[10] Where market price is not obtainable, the attempt of assessors to estimate it often results in multiple and widely varying standards of assessment. Local assessors as a rule are not sufficiently well-informed to approximate market value, equitably, by the capitalization of earnings.

Book value, on the contrary, is easily obtainable from the reports which must be submitted to the assessing officer. Assessment at book value is precise and automatic. It leaves little to the bias of the assessor, prevents arguments,[11] and is more stable than market value.[12] These considerations, coupled with the ease and economy of assessment on this basis, give it a strong appeal to tax officials.

An objection to the use of book value as the basis of assessing

[9] *Report of the Seventh State Conference on Taxation*, Michigan, 1918, pp. 10 ff.; *Report of the Special Commission on Taxation of Corporations*, Conn., 1913, pp. 132 ff.; *Report of Wisconsin Tax Commission*, 1920, pp. 70 ff.; *Report of the Special Commission on Revenue and Taxation*, Neb., 1914, pp. 110 ff.

[10] *Report of Special Commission on Taxation of Corporations*, Conn., 1913, p. 132.

[11] Charles W. Boyden, "Bank and Taxes," *Bul.*, Illinois Bankers Association, April, 1929, p. 13.

[12] *Report of Special Commission on Taxation of Corporations*, Conn., 1913, pp. 132 ff.

the share capital of banks is that it is not true value.[13]   Absolute
equivalence between book and market is not necessary, however,
to secure substantial justice since other property is not assessed
generally at full cash value.   Book value is also objectionable because it is subject to manipulation.   However, it is questionable
if manipulation is sufficiently general to impair seriously the
effectiveness of this method of assessment.[14]   The advantages to
be derived from the use of book value outweigh the objections
which may be urged against it.

Other bases of assessment have been used.   Wyoming uses
par value for the tax base.[15]   This practice has little to commend
it, as there is no consistent relation between par value and invested
capital.   The use of par value tends inevitably to produce serious
discriminations as among banks since few banks have the same
ratio of surplus to capital.[16]

From the assessment base certain deductions are permitted.
Every general property tax state permits some deduction for the
bank's investment in real property.   The legal theory underlying
this deduction is that the taxation of both the shares and the real
property at full value would constitute double taxation, the sup-
position being that the funds of the shareholders, and not those
of the depositor, are invested in real property.[17]   Such deductions
are not required by Section 5219, but rest rather on the tax policy

[13] *Proc., N. T. A.,* 1919, p. 126; *Report of Special Commission on Revenue and Taxation,* Neb., 1914, p. 110; *Report of Special Commission on
the Taxation of Corporations,* Conn., 1913, pp. 132 ff.

[14] *Sixth Report of State Tax Commission,* Arizona, 1922, p. 22.

[15] *Session Laws of 1927,* Wyoming, chap. 75.

[16] See instance of resulting discrimination in *Report of Pennsylvania
Tax Commission,* 1925, p. 15; L. P. Fox, *The Taxation for State Purposes
in Pennsylvania.*

[17] *Prim* v. *Fort,* 57 S. W. 86 (1900); *Smith et al.* v. *Stephens,* 173 Ind.
564 (1909); *State* v. *Butler,* 242 S. W. 979 (1922); *Merchants and Farmers Bank* v. *City of Kosciusko,* 116 S. 88 (1928).

of the individual state.[18] The court has consistently maintained the position that the full value of the shares is taxable to the holder.[19]

The amount of the real estate deduction varies among the several states. Most states permit the deduction of the assessed value of the real estate. Arizona, Louisiana, Missouri, South Carolina, and South Dakota authorize the deduction of the book value of such property. As a general rule, real estate situated outside the state is not deductible for the reason that it is not taxable under the authority of that state and no question of double taxation arises within that jurisdiction.[20] Minnesota permits only the deduction of the legally owned real estate, an amount not in excess of 25 per cent of the capital and surplus of the bank. New Mexico similarly restricts the real property deduction.

Minor discriminations arise from the real estate deduction. In those states which permit state banks to deduct only legally owned real estate, discriminations may arise between state banks and those national banks which hold relatively more real estate than state banks. The deduction of the book value of real estate may produce discriminations as among banks if some banks have written off their real property more rapidly than others. It is hardly to be expected that the rates of depreciation will be uniform as among banks.

A more satisfactory policy with respect to real estate is the deduction of the assessed value. This procedure reduces the discriminations as among banks, if their real property is uniformly assessed, and insures the taxation of the full value of the shares. Since the purpose of the deduction is to prevent double taxation, the subtraction of the assessed value will effect this result. This

[18] *Merchants and Manufacturers Bank* v. *Pennsylvania*, 167 U. S. 461 (1897). Pennsylvania taxes bank shares at 4 mills.

[19] See chap. 3, *supra*.

[20] *Bul.*, N. T. A., 1917, p. 196; *Report of the State Board of Tax Commissioners*, Washington, 1906, p. 197; *Report of the Tax Commission of Kansas*, 1918, p. 160.

plan possesses also the advantages of simplicity and ease of assessment of shares. It removes any pressure to under-value the real property of banks for purposes of taxation. The laws of several states rightly permit the banks to deduct their equity in a bank building subsidiary.

Nevada permits the deduction of the value of all mortgages held by the bank on which it has paid the taxes on the theory that the mortgagee has an interest in the property.[21] The deduction of mortgage loans produces discriminations as between banks which hold such mortgages and those which invest their funds in more liquid assets. It is open to serious question. If loans secured by real estate mortgages are deductible, it would appear reasonable to permit also the deduction of loans secured by chattel mortgages on tangible personalty, loans secured by warehouse receipts to stored commodities, and similar paper, a process which would wipe out in many cases the taxable value of the shares.

Since the share tax is in legal contemplation a tax on the shareholder, West Virginia permits shareholders the deduction of personal debts. Other states have at times followed this procedure. The inevitable effect of this deduction would appear to be discriminatory. The share tax in reality is a levy on the bank, and such deductions only create inequalities as between banks whose stockholders are in debt and banks whose shareholders are debt-free.[22] Some states have solved this conflict between legal and economic categories by defining credits so as to exclude bank shares, while others have prohibited such deductions by statutory provisions. Kansas, Indiana, Iowa, Ohio, and Texas are included in these groups.[23]

[21] *Statutes of 1915,* chap. 174, sec. 3820; *Compiled Laws,* 1930, sec. 6538.
[22] The debts of shareholders are deductible from the total credits of which bank shares are a part.
[23] *Instructions to Assessors,* Kansas, 1928, p. 18; *Laws of Taxation,* Indiana, 1930, pp. 89 ff.; *Laws Relating to Assessment and Taxation,* Iowa, 1930, p. 172; *Report of Tax Commission,* Ohio, 1927, pp. 7 ff.; for Texas see *Prim* v. *Fort,* 57 S. W. 89 (1900).

Another troublesome deduction, unique in the North Carolina law, is the subtraction of a certain percentage of loans and discounts which have been declared uncollectible. There is little logic in this deduction. Intelligently operated banks will provide for such losses through liberal reserves. Hence to permit a deduction of estimated uncollectibles from surplus and undivided profits is in reality a double subtraction from the value of bank shares.

When banks were taxed, prior to 1864, on their capital rather than on their shares, tax exempt securities could not be included in the value of such capital, but, insofar as Section 5219 is concerned, the taxation of the shares of banking institutions does not require the deduction of such property.[24] However, North Carolina,[25] South Carolina,[26] and Michigan still permit deductions of certain tax exempt securities from the value of bank shares. Such deductions can hardly be defended on the grounds of equitable taxation. Some banks by virtue of their location and clientele will carry more deductible securities than others, and likewise enjoy resultingly lower tax burdens. Hence the door is open to substantial discriminations arising out of the character of the operations of the individual bank. It may be urged that such deductions encourage banks to maintain a desirable secondary reserve in readily marketable securities, but discriminatory taxation is not a suitable inducement to extend for this purpose.

New Mexico, South Dakota, and Wyoming do not tax fully the value contributed to bank shares by surplus and undivided profits. The special treatment of the surplus value of shares is effected either by applying a lower nominal rate to surplus or by providing for the exemption of all or a certain percentage of it. Various reasons are advanced for this policy. Banks have generally objected to the taxation of the share value of these items on

[24] See chap. 3, *supra*.
[25] *North Carolina Code of 1931*, sec. 7971.
[26] *Civil Code of South Carolina*, 1922, chap. 15, Art. III, sec. 342; *South Carolina Acts*, 1931, chap. 162.

the ground that it penalized the accumulation of a large invested capital. The favored treatment of surplus may, however, be attributed largely to emergency compromise legislation invoked by the recent decisions of the courts. While defensible as such, these provisions have little else to commend them. Viewed from the standpoint of tax policy, such provisions operate to produce discriminations as between banks which have a large surplus and those which have a small surplus. In effect this has frequently favored the large bank as against the small one. There is no uniform relation between invested capital and tax burden when surplus is accorded favored treatment, as there is no constant ratio between capital and surplus as among banks.

With the exceptions of North Dakota, North Carolina, and New Mexico, general property tax states leave the assessment of bank shares to local assessors. Inequalities in assessment are the well-nigh universal result. The causes for inequitable bank assessments by local officers are not difficult to discover. Ignorance and inexpertness are frequently the chief reasons.[27] Varying standards of assessment, honestly conceived and honestly applied, account for other instances of discriminations. The fact that local assessors, many of them poorly equipped for the task, must assess a huge volume of wealth of myriad types within a very short period makes equitable assessment utterly impossible.[28] Assessors may also reflect the alleged wide-spread prejudice against wealth in assessing banks and other moneyed institutions.[29] Willful and intentional violations of the law by extending favored treatment to friendly banks are matters of record.[30]

[27] *Report of Wisconsin Tax Commission*, 1920, p. 81 ff.; J. C. Mabry, "Bank Taxation, Injustices and Inequalities," *Bank. Mag.*, LIII, 43 ff.; J. H. Fairlie, *A Report on Revenue and Finance Administration*, p. 15.

[28] *Report of Tax Commission to Legislature of Kansas*, 1921, pp. 39 ff.; Fairlie, *op. cit.*, p. 15.

[29] Mabry, *op. cit.*, p. 44.

[30] *Report of the Comptroller General, South Carolina*, 1909, pp. 11 ff.; *ibid.*, 1910, pp. 11 ff.

Tax racketeering has existed if, indeed, it does not now continue.[31]   Excessive tax burdens have been imposed on banks because of mistaken conceptions of the essential nature of banking processes.[32]   Political demagoguery has also exacted its toll on banks.

Several methods of ironing out the inequalities resulting from the assessment of banks by local officials have been tried.   The more precise legal determination of the taxable base by the use of the readily ascertainable book value has helped in reducing discriminations as between banks in certain states.[33]   Local assessment and central revision have contributed to equality of treatment in others.   The state tax officials of Kansas required county assessors to file duplicate copies of bank assessments with them, and efforts were made to smooth out inequalities prior to final equalization by the state board.[34]   The difficulty in central revision usually lies in the limited powers of the equalization boards, some of which are ex officio bodies lacking in adequate power and machinery for effective assessment revision.   Such boards are frequently restricted to the revision of class assessments and have no power to interfere in the valuations of individual tax payers.[35]   No equalization board can make an imperfect original assessment even approximate correctness.[36]

Central assessment has been satisfactorily employed in North Carolina, North Dakota, and New Mexico.   Adequate data for substantially accurate assessment are readily available in the published reports of banks.   It is an economical method of assessment. The assessment of all banks by the same authority tends to insure

[31] Holbrook, "Taxation of Chicago Banks," *Bibliotheca Sacra,* LV, 526-39.

[32] *Bankers Magazine,* LIII, 43 ff.

[33] See *supra.*

[34] *Report of Tax Department, Kansas,* 1928, p. 128.

[35] As for example in Missouri, *State* v. *Harris,* 227 S. W. 818 (1920).

[36] *Report of Tax Commission,* South Dakota, 1916, p. 15.

substantial equality as among banks as superior tax administration may reasonably be expected of state officials. Satisfactory precedents for the central assessment of banks exist in the assessment of public service corporations and railroads. The complete inability of local assessors accurately to value these properties led the states to transfer this work to state boards with results more satisfactory to all parties concerned.

Objections to central assessment rest largely on the contention that equality as between banks and other property may not be secured through the assessment of banks by state officials when other property is assessed by local officers. It is probable none the less that the superior facilities at the command of state officers equip them to adjust relative tax burdens more equitably than can the average local assessor. It may also be urged that central assessment would tend to reduce the interest of bankers in local tax problems to the solution of which their intelligent consideration would contribute. Central assessment, however, constitutes only the initiation of the taxing process. The determination of the local tax rate is quite as important as the assessment ratio, and in the determination of that rate the interest of the bank would still be retained. Moreover, the average banker is usually a man of moderate or substantial wealth, and self-interest would operate to prevent any appreciable diminution of his zeal for equitable taxation. The gains from central assessment more than counterbalance any losses resulting from its use.

Certain conclusions emerge with respect to the assessment of bank shares. More equitable results are obtained when all shares are assessed at the *situs* of the bank, and since the tax is really borne by the bank no valid reason exists for a different practice. Book value is preferable as the tax base because market value is frequently unobtainable, and attempts of assessors to estimate it often result in serious discriminations. Deductions from the

assessment base are also productive of discriminations as among
banks. Where deductions for real estate are allowed, fewer inequalities may be expected if the assessed value, rather than the
book value, of the real property is deducted. This practice is also
in harmony with the legal purpose of the deduction, the prevention
of double taxation. Other deductions in their actual operation
have been provocative of discriminations as among banks, but
have ameliorated the discriminations as between bank shares and
other property in instances where bank shares have been assessed
at a higher ratio of full value than other property. With respect
to the agency of assessment, central assessment is more satisfactory than local assessment.

Any attempt to measure accurately the burden imposed on
bank shares by the general property tax encounters almost insur-
mountable difficulties. Bank assessments are not available except
in local tax duplicates. Varying standards of assessment on the
part of thousands of local assessors render hazardous the process
of sampling. To the assessed valuations state and local tax rates
are applied which are quite as variable for the several tax districts
as are the standards of assessment. The multiplicity of these districts and the inaccessibility of the constantly changing rates further complicate the task of accurate appraisal. With but one
exception, the proceeds of the share taxes on banks are merged
with other items in the reports of tax commissions.

Approximations of the tax burden imposed by the share tax at
general property rates can, however, be made from the assessment
data available in the reports of the tax commissions. Representative assessments throw light on the effectiveness of share taxation. In Arizona for the years, 1920-1928, the ratios of the
assessed value of bank shares to the net book value (the total
book value minus the value of the real property) varied from a
low of 111.0 per cent to a high of 196.6 per cent, the average for
the period being 141.8 per cent. Kansas assessed bank shares at

an average ratio of 99.4 per cent during the years, 1920-1926. The average ratio in Colorado during the period, 1922-1930, was 100.3 per cent. In these states the basis of assessment was full value, and it is apparent that assessing officers enforced the rule. The ratio of share assessment in Minnesota for the years, 1922-1930, was 40.5 per cent. Prior to 1925 the legal basis of valuation was 40.0 per cent for all property. After that date the legal assessment ratio was 33⅓ per cent. The average ratio of assessed value to net book value in Illinois for the years, 1920-1927, was 33.9 per cent, when the legal assessment ratio, save for the last year, was 50.0 per cent. It is, therefore, apparent that bank shares tend to be valued at the full legal rate. This fact constitutes a leading objection which the banks have to share taxation as it is their contention, amply supported by conclusive evidence, that other property is but rarely assessed at full value thereby producing a severe discrimination against banks.

When general property rates are applied to the full value assessment of the share capital of banks, a heavy tax burden necessarily results. Supporting evidence of this is presented in Table III.

Since the accuracy of the basic data on which these computations were made has been vigorously challenged by tax officials, it should be stated that the item "Reported State Taxes" was compiled from the federal income tax returns at the request of representatives of the American Bankers Association and was presented at Congressional hearings in 1930. Unfortunately, the reports of the Commissioner of Internal Revenue do not permit an independent calculation of the questioned item, but such checks as the writer has been able to make from available scattered sources have not revealed discrepancies uniformly favorable to the banks. Moreover, the only other adequate data as to the tax burden imposed by the share tax at general property rates lend support to the substantial accuracy of the estimated burden. Prior to the adoption of the franchise tax, Massachusetts employed

TABLE III. REPORTED STATE TAXES AND NET PROFITS OF
NATIONAL BANKS, 1926*
(In thousands of dollars)

State	Reported state taxes	Net profits for year ending June 30, 1926	Ratio of taxes to net profits
Arizona...................	$ 110	$ 199†	...
Arkansas.................	736	791	93%
Colorado.................	879	1,131	77
Georgia..................	755	1,812	41
Illinois..................	5,693	16,484	33
Iowa....................	884	184	480
Kansas..................	1,113	1,219	91
Louisiana................	765	1,407	54
Michigan................	1,749	5,042	34
Minnesota...............	1,764	4,688	37
Mississippi..............	418	909	46
Missouri.................	1,674	5,271	31
Montana.................	210	411	51
New Mexico.............	112	52	215
North Carolina..........	385	1,995	19
North Dakota............	279	110	253
South Carolina..........	496	388	128
South Dakota............	157	62	253
Tennessee...............	808	2,465	32
Texas...................	3,379	11,098	30
West Virginia............	564	1,908	29
Wyoming................	126	252	50

*Computed from *Report of Comptroller of Currency*, 1926, and reported taxes for federal income tax returns as shown in House *Hearings*, 1930, pp. 30 ff.
†Deficit.

share taxation. During the period, 1913-1922, share taxes on national banks in that state averaged 25.8 per cent of net income varying from 17.9 per cent in 1917 to 44.3 per cent in 1922.[37] The evidence is persuasive that the share taxation at general property rates imposes a very severe burden on banks when the shares are assessed at full value. Banks in many states undoubtedly have been the victims of heavy taxation, all too frequently discriminatory in character.[38]

[37] Compiled from *Report of the Comptroller of Currency* and *Reports of the Commissioner of Corporations and Taxation*.

[38] Numerous instances of such discriminations against banks in the general property tax states abound in the reports of tax commissions, proceedings of various state bankers associations, and in Congressional hearings.

The explanation for this heavy, and at times discriminatory, taxation of bank shares at general property rates is not difficult. Assessment at book value is easily consummated. Collection at the source is equally facile. Banks have too frequently been thought of as reservoirs of immense wealth, profitable beyond the imagination of the local assessor, and hence amply able to bear the burdens imposed. The narrow margin of profit which banks make on each dollar of assets is not understood by the public. Indeed the nature of the banking process itself is such as to lead the average man into believing that an individual bank can in some mysterious way make a dollar of primary deposits multiply itself into some ten dollars of earning assets—for does not the bank have to keep a reserve of only 10 per cent? Popular confusion of the credit multiplication possible in the banking system with the limited expansibility of the credit of the individual bank has doubtless played its part in the excessive tax burden imposed on banks.

Not all of the discriminations against banks can be laid at the door of ill-informed assessors. Shrewd politicians have at times capitalized the inarticulate prejudice against the money lender in a democratic state. The cry against the "money interests" has quite frequently received a sympathetic response in heavier tax burdens on those institutions which were, prior to the depression, synonymous with money.

From these discriminations the bankers in some states sought relief by direct appeal to local assessing officers supported by periodic tests in the courts. In Missouri and Illinois, particularly, well directed campaigns by the banking associations produced substantial, if not satisfactory, relief.[39] In other states changes from the taxation of share capital at general property rates to a uniform rate, usually considerably lower than the general property

[39] *Proceedings,* of the Missouri Bankers Association, 1905, 1911, 1922, 1924-1928; Illinois Bankers Association *Bulletin,* IX, 19.

tax levy, resulted in measurable relief. Tax nullification through judicial appeal under the protective clause of the federal statute, while undoubtedly carried beyond reasonable limits, has been none the less a logical offspring of the discriminatory exactions from banks.   In still other states efforts to reduce the burden on banks by centralized assessment have produced beneficial results.

Discriminations, actual or alleged, are not the only basis of opposition to the general property tax method. It is contended that it retards and penalizes the bank in building up an adequate surplus, thus leading to an inadequate amount of invested capital to support the deposit liabilities of the bank.[40]   That these results have been experienced in individual cases cannot be seriously questioned, but it is doubtful whether they have been general or substantial.   Comparison of the invested capital of national banks to total assets and to total deposits for the years, 1915-1922, in Massachusetts where bank shares were heavily taxed and in Pennsylvania where a low millage rate obtained, showed no striking divergences.   Factors other than taxation are more important in determining the ratio of net worth to deposit liabilities.

Another charge levelled at share taxation of banks is that it has appreciably contributed to bank failures. For this claim there is but little support.   Since the Richmond decision in 1921 bank

[40] Since this study was completed the National Industrial Conference Board has published, *The Taxation of Banks,* which deals in more detail with the effects of taxation on banking operations.   Evidence is there adduced (chap. 6) to support the view that share taxation has operated to impair seriously the capital structure of banks.   It is not to be denied that any expense such as taxes, wages, salaries, or interest reduces the net income of banks and tends to restrict the reinvestment of earnings, but the present writer does not share the opinion that taxes, which during the years, 1925-1931, never exceeded 8.2 per cent of the total expenses of national banks (Table 27 of the above study), were of sufficient moment to reduce seriously the ratio of invested capital to deposits.   The declining ratio of invested capital to assets since 1913 was, as Professor Hardy has shown in, *Credit Policies of the Federal Reserve System,* chap. 17, a world-wide tendency which in this country was but little influenced by the tax burden imposed on banks.

taxes have been greatly reduced. In several states compromise taxation obtains. Yet during this period when the state tax burden on banks has been the lightest, the tide of bank failures reached historic proportions. Bank failures have been due to much more potent factors than the share tax burden. Multiple banking systems, loosely supervised, permitted the excessive multiplication of fair-weather banks which were too frequently improperly managed by inexperienced bankers. Such institutions could not stand the strain of agricultural depression and a world economic recession. That bank taxes may have been a minor contributing element in individual banks is within the realm of possibility, but taxation is not a feasible explanation of the recent avalanche of bank failures.

A further objection to the taxation of bank shares at general property rates is that it is not in harmony with the faculty principle. In this respect the taxation of bank shares is not unique. There is, however, a close relation over a period of years between the tax burden on bank shares assessed at book value and bank earnings. Earnings not paid out in dividends are reinvested in the business and are directly reflected in the increasing book value of the bank. While the taxation of bank shares may do considerable violence to the faculty principle in a given year or for individual banks over a period of years, it is not substantially inconsistent with the faculty principle as applied to the business of banking over a period of time.

From the standpoint of the states the virtue of share taxation at general property rates is its productivity. The yield of the general property tax on shares has proved greater in practice than the revenues derived from other methods of bank taxation. It has produced from three to five times the revenues obtained by the states using excise and income taxation.[41] As compared with the returns received from the taxation of bank shares at a uni-

[41] See chap. 6, *supra.*

form rate, the general property tax method is generally the more productive. Indeed, a uniform rate on bank shares has been frequently adopted as a tax reduction measure. There is of course no reason why the flat rate on bank shares could not be made to yield quite as much as the general property tax method, but as actually employed, it has not resulted in revenues equal to those obtained from the general property tax.[42]

The essential simplicity of share taxation at local rates also commends itself to tax officials. Bank shares are a very homogeneous type of property; the book value of such property is easily obtained from the published reports of banks. Evasion is extremely difficult, if not impossible. Assessment and collection at the source are convenient and inexpensive. No elaborate machinery of administration is required to define rules of assessment or methods of review such as are required in income and excise taxation. Productivity, simplicity, economy, and ease in administration give to share taxation at local rates a powerful appeal to tax administrators. Needless to add it is these very virtues which too frequently have become its vices. Excessive burdens have been imposed on banks in many instances because of the ease of assessment and collection.

[42] See chap. 8, *infra*.

CHAPTER VIII

THE UNIFORM RATE ON BANK SHARES

THE first direct bank tax imposed by any American state was a levy of 2½ per cent imposed by Georgia in 1805 on the capital stock of banks. During the period prior to 1864, other states, among them North Carolina, Massachusetts, Wisconsin, and Delaware employed a uniform rate on banking capital or on bank shares. After the National Bank Act of 1864, share taxation became universal and a number of states adopted the plan of taxing bank shares at a uniform rate. Pennsylvania was among the first to take this step. Following the multiple taxation of banks on their shares, capital, and dividends, this state dropped the levies on dividends and capital, and by 1867 only bank shares remained taxable at a rate of one per cent on their par value. The Act of 1897 changed the state rate to four mills on market value or at an optional rate of ten mills on par value.[1] In 1925 the optional tax was eliminated in order to secure equality of intangible taxation.[2]

The example set by Pennsylvania had considerable influence on neighboring states. The bankers in New York by a forthright presentation of their case succeeded in 1901 in getting the legislature to change the tax on banks to a uniform rate of one per cent, which act continued in force until its nullification and the adoption of the franchise tax.[3] Maryland also adopted the uniform rate of one per cent in 1914 partly to place its banks on a competitive basis with Pennsylvania.[4] New Jersey in the same year shifted from the taxation of bank shares at general property

[1] F. M. Eastman, *Taxation for State Purposes in Pennsylvania* (Kay and Brother, 1898), pp. 93 ff.

[2] *Public Laws of 1925*, chap. 497.

[3] For details of this contest see *American Banker*, LXV, 142; *ibid.*, LXVI, 826 ff.; *Bankers Magazine*, LXI, 249-54, 172.

[4] *Com. and Fin. Chron.*, XCVIII, 128.

rates to a uniform rate of three-fourths of one per cent.[5] Virginia followed suit in 1915 which act, with later changes, brought the rate down to one per cent.[6]

Other states have from time to time adopted this method. At present it is employed by fifteen states. The chief features of the laws of these states are summarized in Table IV. A number of variations exist in these laws. Many of the issues raised by these provisions are similar to those discussed in the preceding chapter and need not be repeated. With respect to the place of assessment, business *situs* is generally followed. Book value constitutes the basis of assessment in Delaware, Indiana, Pennsylvania, Ohio, and Virginia, and is used as a guide in the determination of the taxable value in the other states with the exception of New Hampshire which employs par value as the tax base. The assessment of bank shares is generally vested in state officials, while in

TABLE IV. THE TAXATION OF BANK SHARES AT A UNIFORM RATE

STATE— Legal Citation	Basis of Assessment	Deductions	Tax Rate	Basis of Tax Distribution
CONNECTICUT Gen. Stat. 1930, ch. 67, s. 1272; P. A. 1931, ch. 67.	Fair market value	Real estate taxes from share tax	1%	Residents, towns of residence; nonresidents, to *situs* of bank for natl. banks; other banks to state treasury. Shares, if over 50%, held by corporation or trustee to *situs* of bank.
DELAWARE Laws of Delaware 1921, ch. 104.	Book value	None	1/5 of 1%	To state.
FLORIDA Laws 1931, ch. 15789.	True value	Assessed value of real property	.2 of 1%	State.
INDIANA Acts 1933, ch. 83.	Book value	Book value of real estate	1/4 of 1%	State and locality pro-rata to real estate levies.

[5] *Report of Board of Equalization*, 1914, pp. 17 ff.
[6] *Tax Code of Virginia*, 1930, chap. 8, sec. 91.

STATE— Legal Citation	Basis of Assessment	Deductions	Tax Rate	Basis of Tax Distribution
IOWA Code, s. 6989, 7003; 45 G. A., ch. 86.	Actual value	Investment in real estate or equity in building subsidiary	.5 of 1% .1 of 1% additional until 1942	State and localities.
KENTUCKY Carroll's Stat. 1930, s. 4092, 4019.	Fair cash value	Assessed value of real estate	State .5 of 1% County .2 of 1% City .2 of 1% School .4 of 1%	To several jurisdictions on basis of rates im- posed.
MAINE Rev. Stat. 1930, ch. 12, s. 76-78; Laws 1931, ch. 253.	Just value	Assessed value of real estate	1.5%	Residents, towns of resi- dence; nonresidents and shares owned by corporations, to *situs* of bank.
MARYLAND Laws of 1929, ch. 226.	Market, but not less than book value	1. Assessed value of real estate. 2. As- sessed value of natl. bank stock held for 6 months. 3. Balti- more stock and cer- tain corporate shares	Local rate of 1% plus state rate on property	To state and localities on basis of rates im- posed.
NEBRASKA Laws 1933, ch. 130.	True value, book as guide	Assessed value of real and tangible property	1%	1/6 to state, 5/6 to localities.
NEW HAMPSHIRE Public Laws 1926, ch. 70; Laws 1933 ch. 115.	Par value	Value of real estate	1%	Residents, town of resi- dence; nonresidents to *situs* of bank.
NEW JERSEY Tax Laws 1926; Sup. to Comp. Stat. s. 208-500a.	True value based on book value	Assessed value of real property	3/4 of 1%	1/2 to county, 1/2 to local district.
OHIO Laws 1931, ch. 114; Laws 1933, Amend- ed S. B. 30.	Book value	None	.2 of 1%	To localities.
PENNSYLVANIA Purdon's Stat. T.72, s. 1931 ff.; Laws 1933, Act 277.	Book value	None	.4 of 1%	To state.
RHODE ISLAND Tax Laws 1930, pp. 95-98.	Fair cash value	Assessed value of real estate	.4 of 1%	To municipalities.
VIRGINIA Va. Tax Code 1930, s. 89-97; 1934 Sup. s. 97 a b.	Book value	Assessed value of real estate, or equity in building subsidiary	1%	City may share 40%, town 80%, balance to state.

New Hampshire, Kentucky, and Virginia review by state tax officials tends to produce uniformity in assessment ratios.

Certain variations occur in the deductions permitted from the assessment base. In Pennsylvania, Delaware, and Ohio no deductions are allowed. In the other states the real estate deduction is found, or as in Connecticut, real estate taxes are deductible from the share taxes. The subtractions authorized by the states using the uniform rate are not nearly so numerous or troublesome as those allowed by many of the general property tax states.[7] Discriminations as among banks are thereby reduced.

The most important variations are found in the nominal tax rates and in the distribution of the revenues. With respect to the nominal rate, Florida, Ohio, and Delaware, with a levy of two mills, have the lowest, and Kentucky with a combined state and local levy of 1.3 per cent has the highest. There is no uniformity in the distribution of the revenues. In Pennsylvania, Florida, and Delaware the proceeds go to the state treasury. In Connecticut, Maine, and New Hampshire the proceeds from the shares held by residents accrue to the towns in which the shareholders reside, while the revenues from the shares held by nonresidents go to the town in which the bank is located. Maryland, Kentucky, Nebraska, Indiana, Iowa, and Virginia split the funds between the state and local governments on a stipulated basis, as do also New Jersey and Rhode Island. In Ohio the receipts accrue to the localities except for a small charge for state administration. With few exceptions the tax is not strictly a state levy.

Data are not available to determine the relative tax burden on banks in most of the uniform rate states, but a few comparisons may be made. State and local taxes levied on corporations in Pennsylvania in 1923 varied, averaging 1.28 per cent of invested capital as compared with a rate of four-tenths of one per cent on

[7] See chap. 7, *supra*.

bank shares.[8]   Reduced to an income basis state and local taxes
on Pennsylvania corporations absorbed 9.53 per cent of net income as compared with an estimated share tax burden of 4.53
per cent of the net income of banks.[9]   If to share taxes are added
the real property levies imposed on banks, approximate equality
of tax burden is obtained.

The average tax burden on corporations in Connecticut in
1928 equalled .849 of one per cent of total assets, 1.566 per cent
of invested capital, and 28.6 per cent of net income before taxes
while the levies on national banks amounted to .222 of one per
cent of total assets, 1.33 per cent of invested capital, and 15.0
per cent of comparable net income, thus indicating that national
banks in that year were less heavily taxed than other corporations.[10]   A Virginia tax official holds that the present rate of one
per cent on banks approximates the tax burden on other corporations.   Estimates of the share tax levies in other states are
persuasive of reasonable, and in some instances, notably Delaware,
Ohio, Indiana, Florida, and New Hampshire, very light impositions.   (See Table V.)

Though the evidence is not conclusive, it is persuasive that the
uniform rate has operated with substantial justice to banks.   Cer-

TABLE V. ESTIMATED SHARE TAX BURDENS

State	Period	Taxes to Book Value (Average)	Taxes to Net Profits (Average)
Delaware	1924–1929	0.151%	....
Maine*	1922–1928	.74	8.88
Maryland	1922–1928	1.09	....
New Hampshire*	1923–1929	.32	5.58
New Jersey	1922–1928	.58	....

Computed from *Reports of Tax Commissions* and *Reports of the Comptroller of Currency*. Absence of
income data for state banks prohibits income tests in Delaware, Maryland, and New Jersey.
*For national banks only.

[8] *Final Report of the Pennsylvania Tax Commission*, 1927, p. 123.
[9] Computed from *Report of Comptroller of Currency*, 1924.
[10] Data secured from State Tax Commissioner.

tainly banks cannot claim that they are excessively taxed, nor can the states, in many instances, support the charge of fiscal inadequacy for the uniform rate method.

Significant advantages characterize this method of bank taxation. It has all but eliminated discriminations as among banks and has substantially circumscribed the discriminations as between banks and other corporations. The uniform rate harmonizes substantially with the nature of the banking process. Local tax jurisdictions do not coincide with the sphere of banking operations. Since some governmental unit must determine the tax rate, it may be urged that the most appropriate unit to perform this function is the state. An alternative to this is the determination of the rate by the locality, but a reasonable regard for the nature of the banking process and recent trends in banking organization cast serious doubts on the advisability of this method. The determination by the state of a uniform rate on bank shares offers a reasonable compromise solution. It extends to all banks within the state substantial equality of treatment and prevents large metropolitan banks, taxed at low effective rates, from enjoying any unfair competitive advantage over small banking institutions located in higher tax jurisdictions.

The administrative advantages of the uniform rate method of taxing bank shares are apparent. Assessment by more expert appraisers, collection in some instances by state officials, and review by central boards in the few states where original assessments are made by local assessors combine to make this method administratively economical and effective.

The taxation of bank shares at a uniform rate has frequently resulted in a more equitable treatment of banks as compared with other property. Its evolution in a number of states reflects a definite attempt to remove the discriminations between banks and other property. That the taxation of banks at a uniform rate always establishes equality as between banks and other property cannot be maintained. In some states employing this method banks may enjoy a favored position in the tax system. There is nothing in the uniform rate which intrinsically guarantees substantial equality. The rate may indeed be fixed at a point which will either over-tax or under-tax banks. Notwithstanding this consideration, the inescapable fact that the rate adopted must be accorded the deliberate attention of the state legislature removes the banks from the caprice of local officials who may be inclined either to favor or frown upon these institutions.

States employing a uniform tax rate on bank shares have had relatively less bank tax litigation than has been found in the general property states, though the voidability of the uniform taxes in a number of states is generally known. Upon the whole, the fixed rate has appealed to many bankers as a reasonably equitable method of taxing bank shares, and they have given it their substantial support in most states. New York and California constitute notable exceptions to this rule. The fact that banks have given substantial support to the uniform rate in most states which have employed this method of bank taxation is not conclusive evidence that the fixed rate in practice has operated with justice to all tax payers. It is valuable testimony, none the less, to the fact that banks, which have too frequently felt the burden of discriminatory taxation in the general property tax states, believe the uniform rate a more equitable form of taxation.

Objections to the uniform rate on bank shares rest broadly on three bases. In the first place it may be urged that banks are local institutions whose primary obligation is to the tax jurisdiction in which the bank is situated. This thesis is clearly open to question. The widening territorial area in which the average bank operates and the increasing urbanization of the population, which has changed the relative importance of previously determined tax jurisdictions, though difficult to measure objectively, qualify appreciably the assumption of financial provinciality. Adequate protection of the local interest is generally obtained in the distribution of the revenues which is of course the chief consideration.

The second objection is that it may not accord justice either to the banks or to other taxpayers. It may favor the banks, particularly in states where the rates on other property are rapidly rising. There is merit in this consideration as the rate, once established, tends to be perpetuated. No changes in the maximum rate have been made in Pennsylvania since 1897; the one per cent rate was retained in New York from 1901 to 1926, and in Connecticut it has been in effect since 1901. In Maryland no change in the uniform local rate has been made since its adoption, and the rate of three-fourths of one per cent has continued in New Jersey since 1914. During this period rates on other property have been advanced appreciably.

Constancy in the rate over a period of time is not, however, a necessary characteristic of this method of taxation. The rate on bank shares may be adjusted progressively to the changes in relative tax burden on other property without losing any of the advantageous features which inhere in its use. California changed its rate on banks three times in the effort to equalize the burden between banks and other corporations, and, though the banks protested, the evidence is persuasive that they had no serious grievance. A uniform rate may thus be adjusted to changes in the tax burden on other subjects.

The third objection to the uniform rate is that it is discriminatory when measured by the income test. Large banks may be more lightly taxed than small banks due to the greater relative profits of the larger institutions. Obviously a property tax is not an income tax, and its equality cannot be determined by the income test. Since this criticism of the uniform rate is alike applicable to all property taxation, the several states which without exception employ some type of property taxation cannot be condemned for its application to banks so long as unreasonable discriminations do not exist.

It should be noted, in conclusion, that legal difficulties may present themselves in the adoption of the uniform rate in some states where the uniformity clause of the constitution is rigidly applied. Such an eventuality depends on the viewpoint of the several state supreme courts. In some states the uniformity clause has not obstructed its use. The New Jersey court held that the classification of banks for taxation at the uniform rate of three-fourths of one per cent was not a violation of the uniformity provision due to the unique nature of the banking process.[11] A recent decision by the United States Supreme Court also indicates the validity of the classification of banks for tax purposes.[12] As long as classification for tax purposes has been reasonable, has been made in good faith, has been sustained by inherent differences in the nature of the business, and has not created arbitrary inequalities, even though some injustice may be done by the classification, the courts have tended to sustain the tax categories established by the legislature.[13] Apparently, some states can hurdle the uniformity clause and the Fourteenth Amendment if they desire to classify banks and impose on them a uniform rate.

With respect to the present inhibitions of Section 5219, the uniform rate on bank shares offers no complete solution. The rate as fixed by the legislature may or may not correspond with that imposed on competing moneyed capital. In most states the rate on banks is higher than that levied on certain forms of other moneyed capital. As a matter of fact, the banks so far have not been so inclined to contest the uniform rate as they have the taxes imposed on bank shares in the general property tax states. Perhaps in bank taxation past experience is as valuable a guide as it is in other fields of human relations.

[11] *Commercial Trust Co.* v. *Hudson County Board of Education,* 92 Atl. Rep. 800 (1915).

[12] *Union Bank and Trust Co.* v. *Phelps,* 288 U. S. 181 (1933).

[13] Cooley, *Taxation* (4th ed.), Vol. I, Art. 334.

CHAPTER IX

THE DISPROPORTIONATE TAXATION OF
STATE BANKS

IN January, 1899, the editor of a leading American banking journal proposed the uniform taxation of all banks to be effected by a federal statute which would standardize the taxes on national banks and thereby induce the states to apply the same method to state institutions.[1] The bankers have repeatedly asserted that Section 5219 tends to produce this effect.[2] While state banks have shared the protection of the sheltering arm of the federal statute, there are, nevertheless, twenty-one states which impose additional taxes on state banks which Section 5219 prohibits on national institutions. The character and extent of this disproportionate taxation of state banks are summarized in Table VI.[3]

The burden imposed by these taxes varies from relatively light franchise levies on capital to heavier taxes on either gross or net income. In Indiana and South Dakota gross income taxes of one per cent raise appreciably the burden on state banks, as does also the present nine-twentieths of one per cent tax in West Virginia. The tax on net income of two per cent in Arkansas and Missouri, six per cent in North Carolina, and the excise tax of three per cent of net income in Tennessee also add a substantial additional burden on state institutions. Three states, Arkansas, Missouri, and West

---

[1] *Bank Magazine,* LVIII, 15-17.

[2] A. B. A. *Journal,* XIV, 622; House *Hearings,* 1922, pp. 112, 220 ff.; A. B. A. *Commercial and Financial Chronicle,* Supplement, 1927, p. 84; *ibid.,* 1928, p. 82.

[3] Fees paid by state banks to cover the costs of state banking departments represent expenditures for services rendered and are not included in this discussion. Similarly, non-recurring incorporation fees are likewise excluded.

TABLE VI. SUPPLEMENTARY TAXES ON STATE BANKS

State	Legal Citation	Tax
Alabama..........	*Gen. Acts*, 1927, No. 163 *Gen. Acts*, 1931, No. 278	Franchise tax $2 per $1000 on capital; after 1935 $1 per $1000.
Arkansas..........	*C. & M. Digest Stat. of Ark.* Supplement of 1925; *Acts* 1929, No. 118, s. 3.	1. License tax 11/100 of 1% of out-standing stock domestically em-ployed. 2. Income tax of 2%.
Colorado..........	*Comp. Laws*, 1921, s. 7270, 7278	Franchise tax $10 on first $100,000 capital plus 10 cents on each addi-tional $1000.
Florida...........	*Tax Laws*, 1930, s. 1095	License tax $10 per $10,000 capital
Idaho............	*Idaho Code*, 1932, s. 29-603	License tax graduated $10 per $5000 capital to $150 for capital in excess of $2,000,000.
Indiana..........	*Acts*, 1933, Ch. 50, s. 1, 3	Gross income tax of 1%.
Louisiana........	*Gen. Stat.*, 1932, s. 8590	License tax on book value of capital; graduated in 92 classes from $50 on $25,000 to $76,000 on $75,000,000 or more.
Michigan.........	*Comp. Laws*, Ch. 196, s. 10140	Privilege fee of 2½ mills on capital and surplus.
Missouri.........	*Laws*, 1931, H. B. 183; *Laws*, 1929, S. B. 480	1. Income tax of 2%. 2. Franchise tax 1/20 of 1% on out-standing capital and surplus.
Montana.........	*Rev. Code*, 1921, s. 2296ff	License tax of 1% of net income.
North Carolina....	*Public Laws*, 1933, Ch. 445, s. 311	Income tax of 6%.
Ohio.............	*Throckmorton's Code*, 1929, s. 5498-99	Franchise fee of 1 mill on book value
Oregon...........	*Code*, 1930, s. 25-237	License tax graduated from $10 for $5000 authorized capital to $200 for over $2,000,000.
Rhode Island.....	*Tax Laws*, 1930, p. 89	Franchise tax $2.50 per $10,000 au-thorized capital.
South Dakota.....	*Sess. Laws*, 1933, Ch. 184	Gross income tax of 1%.
Texas............	*Rev. Civil Stat.*, 1931, Art. 7084	Franchise tax on capital, at book value, 60 cents per $1000 up to $1,000,000. 30 cents per $1000 in excess of $1,000,000.

State	Legal Citation	Tax
Tennessee........	*Code of 1932*, s. 1316-28	Excise tax of 3% of net income; may use as credit for privilege tax.
Vermont.........	Public Laws, 1933 (Proposed Revision), s. 916-19	Annual license on capital or deposits graduated from $10 to $100.
Washington......	*Remington's Rev. Stat.*, 1933, Title 25, Ch. 1, s. 3836	Annual license fee on authorized capital stock graduated $15 for first $50,000. Maximum tax $1250.
West Virginia.....	*Acts* Extra Sess., 1933, Chap. 66; *Code of 1931*, s. 17-13-2d; 11-12-69	1. Gross income tax 3/10 of 1%; surtax of 3/20 until June 30, 1935. 2. Graduated license tax of $20 on $5000 capital to $2500 for more than $15,000,000.
Wyoming........	*Rev. Stat.*, 1931, s. 28-1001	License tax for capital and assets in Wyoming. Graduated $5 for first $50,000 to $50 for each $1,000,000.

Virginia, impose two additional taxes on state banks which cannot be legally exacted from national banks.

To these taxes imposed on state banks should be added the inequalities resulting from the invalidation of national bank taxes in a number of states. While these were being ironed out through compromise legislation, they temporarily subjected state institutions to a tax disadvantage. Bond deductions in some states have also operated to impose a disproportionate burden on state banks.

The reasons are patent for the heavier taxation by certain states of banks of their own creation. Prominent among them is the inflexibility of Section 5219. Under the federal statute, national banks cannot be taxed both on property and on income. Since several states resort to both property and income taxation on other corporations, Section 5219 unduly circumscribes them in the taxation of national banks. The state is faced with the alternatives of taxing state banks at a higher rate through multiple levies than it may legally impose on national banks, or the taxation of other corporations at a higher rate than is imposed on state banks. Under such conditions fiscal necessity may be the deciding issue, in which case the state bank is generally brought within the scope of the income tax.

The disproportionate taxation of state banks naturally raises serious legal questions as to the validity of tax classifications. In South Dakota[4] and Nebraska[5] the local courts extended to state banks the immunity from share taxes which the national banks had won. But a contrary view was held by the Alabama court which was in turn sustained by the United States Supreme Court.[6] In this decision, which may be suggestive of a more liberal position, the court said:

There is nothing to indicate that Congress ever supposed that mere establishment of a National Bank within a State could upset the scheme, theretofore entirely proper, by producing conflict with the XIV Amendment. This view would subject the taxing power of the State to the will of Congress far beyond what is necessary for the protection of Federal agencies. The Constitutional inhibition against taxing these agencies does not abridge the taxing power of the several states in respect of other property.[7]

The preceding pages bear persuasive testimony to the contention that Section 5219 has in the past modified the tax structures of several states with respect to other tax subjects. Whether its circumscribing influence constitutes an abridgment of the taxing power of the state, obviously the court alone can determine. The layman can only salute the position taken in the Alabama case and hope for an interpretation of the restrictive provision of the federal statute which, within the limits of that law, will allow the state the maximum freedom.

With respect to the essential justice of equality of tax burden as between state and national banks little need be said. They are

[4] *Commercial State Bank* v. *Wilson,* 220 N. W. 152 (1928).
[5] *State Bank* v. *Endres,* 192 N. W. 322 (1923).
[6] *Union Bank and Trust Company* v. *Phelps,* 288 U. S. 181 (1933).
[7] *Ibid.,* p 187.

engaged in substantially similar operations and possess substantially equal powers. Approximate parity of competitive power demands practical equality in tax burden. Some observers have professed the view that the difference in state tax status would lead to the forced nationalization of state banks, but there is no conclusive evidence to support this hypothesis.[8] National banking resources have, it is true, increased relative to state commercial banking assets since 1921, the assets of federal institutions comprising 59 per cent of total commercial banking assets in 1921, 61 per cent in 1927, 62 per cent in 1929, and 72 per cent in 1933. While state taxation may have contributed in a minor way to this trend, the more significant factors in the situation have been the increased prerogatives which national banks obtained in the Mc-Fadden Act of 1927, and the higher mortality rate of state banks.[9] State tax considerations cannot be disregarded in the choice of a charter but they are rarely controlling factors for banks.

[8] See House *Hearings* 1922, pp. 79, 111-15, 118-19, 140-44; *ibid.*, 1928, p. 58; Senate *Hearings* 1928, pp. 23, 87.

[9] See B. W. Goldschmidt, *The Changing Structure of American Banking* (London: Rutledge, 1933), chap. 10.

CHAPTER X

A SUGGESTED SOLUTION FOR THE BANK
TAX PROBLEM

IN VIEW of the limited statistical data as to the taxes imposed on banks by the states, perhaps the best way to compare the methods of taxation now employed is through the device of applying assumed rates to the average national bank for the more normal year of 1928. The average national bank in that year had invested capital of $464,307, real estate of $110,116, net profits of $35,126, and total assets of $3,706,701.[1] An income tax of 6 per cent would yield $1,405, under the reasonable assumption that one-third of its net profits was derived from tax exempt sources. A franchise tax of 5 per cent would produce $1,756. A uniform rate of 1 per cent on bank shares, assuming a deduction for the assessed value of the real estate at the rate of 75 per cent of book value, would yield $3,817, or 10.8 per cent of the net income of the bank. If the bank shares were taxed at general property rates of 2.5 per cent, the resultant yield would be $9,543, or 27 per cent of the net income. Assuming that the real estate was assessed at 75 per cent of book value and was subject to a tax rate of $2\frac{1}{2}$ per cent, the ratio of total share and real estate taxes to net income under the several options would be: income, 9.8 per cent; excise, 10.8 per cent; uniform rate, 16.7 per cent; general property, 33.0 per cent.

When similar estimates are made for the average national bank in New York City and the average national bank in North Dakota, striking differences in tax burden appear as is shown in Table VII.

These marked variations are explained by the larger relative holdings of real estate by the banks in North Dakota and the

[1] *Report of the Comptroller of Currency*, 1928, pp. 90 ff.

[125]

TABLE VII. ESTIMATED TAX BURDEN ON AVERAGE NATIONAL BANKS IN 1928

Method and Rate	NEW YORK CITY		NORTH DAKOTA	
	Business Tax to Income	Total Taxes to Income	Business Tax to Income	Total Taxes to Income
Income 6%.......	4.0%	6.0%	3.9%	36.1%
Excise 5%........	5.0	7.0	5.0	36.5
Uniform rate 1%..	11.5	13.5	21.7	53.3
General Property..	28.7	30.7	54.5	86.0

relatively larger profits of the national banks in New York City. When real estate taxes are excluded the differences, though reduced, are still striking. These comparisons emphasize the limits of income as a sole measure of tax burden and the different results which would flow from the application of the same rates on banks of different size, location, earning power, and asset composition.

Further comparisons of the average burden on national banks with the state and local taxes on other corporations throw some light on the question as to whether banks are taxed higher than other business. The average state and local corporate tax burden in the United States, as measured by income, was estimated to be 19.3 per cent in 1922 and 18.8 per cent in 1924.[2] In the light of these facts the following conclusions seem tenable. The taxation of banks on their income or franchise, under existing limitations, fails appreciably to impose a burden on banks which is formally equal to that levied on other corporations. When the additional considerations of the special governmental sanctions thrown around banks are duly weighed, the relative inequality of burden under excise and income taxation becomes more pronounced.

It is equally certain that the taxation of bank shares at general property rates frequently discriminates against banks by virtue of their full assessment when other property is assessed at a lower ratio of actual worth. The general property tax operates with

[2] *Fiscal Problem in New York,* pp. 114 ff.

particular severity on banks.   This discrimination is ameliorated in some states by deductions allowed banks but these deductions create inequalities as among banks.[3]

The uniform rate on banks as employed by fifteen states has proved in practice the most satisfactory compromise method of bank taxation.[4]   Unfortunately, the validity of these taxes in a number of states is dubious.   The undisguised fact is that national banks cannot now be taxed with certainty and adequacy.   They are, and for several years have been, a favored group in the tax system, actually in many states, potentially in other states.   It has been suggested that they are enjoying a "tax holiday" after years of unjust taxation.[5]   There is imperative need, therefore, for a revision of Section 5219.   In such an amendment the states should be accorded a sufficient degree of freedom properly to adjust the taxation of banks to the tax structures which are commonly accepted as proper for them.   Substantial variations in the productive resources, the fiscal requirements, the historical background and the economic organization of the several states demand variety in tax structures.   It is idle to contend that a tax system suitable for industrialized Massachusetts will fit the agricultural pattern of North Dakota.   The federal permissive statute should not in fact as well as in law abridge or seriously circumscribe the taxing power of states with respect to subjects other than national banks.   The preceding pages have indicated the numerous ways in which the present federal statute operates to circumscribe the state taxing policies with respect to other subjects.   At the same time it is incumbent on Congress to accord the proper degree of protection to the national banking organization.   It is doubtful if the Fourteenth Amendment adequately protects national banks from potentially inimical state taxation;

[3] See chap. 7, *supra*.
[4] See chap. 8, *supra*.
[5] *Proc.* N. T. A., 1930, 278.

not, however, because the states maliciously attempt to bleed the banks, but rather because the operative provisions of a share tax which permits assessment and collection at the source in practice frequently result in discriminatory burdens on banks. Appeals to the courts can reduce but not eliminate these discriminations.

The incorporation of these complex considerations into a simple tax formula is clearly a difficult, if not impossible, task. Hence the ever-recurring *impasse* which has featured the several Congressional hearings called to solve the bank tax puzzle. Solutions acceptable to Minnesota have not been favored by Connecticut. Proposals attractive to tax administrators have been frowned on by the banks. Forty-eight states and forty-nine banking systems, manifestly, can hardly be expected to agree on a state tax clause, as thirteen years of keen, and at times bitter, controversy has shown. It is not expected, therefore, that the avowedly compromise suggestion here offered is free from objectionable features nor capable of completely logical defense. It does, however, possess certain virtues and is suggested by the results of the methods now employed. It is proposed simply that the several states shall be permitted to tax (a) the real property of national banks as other real property is taxed and (b) that the shares of such banks may be taxed by and under state authority subject to the limits that the rate imposed shall not exceed an agreed per cent, say, 1½ per cent, of the book value of said shares minus the assessed value of the real property, nor shall the rate be higher than that imposed by the taxing state on banks operating under state charters. That such a proposal falls within the constitutional powers of Congress, the court has already indicated.[6] There remains, therefore, for consideration the advantages of and objections to the compromise plan.

Be it said, initially, that past experience with bank taxation, as heretofore analyzed, lends substantial support to the proposal.

[6] *People* v. *Weaver*, 100 U. S. 539 (1879).

In practice the states with a uniform rate have been able to impose fiscally productive taxes on bank shares and the banks have not, as a general rule, been contentious about their payment. On the whole they have considered the burdens so imposed as reasonable and just.

In the second place, the uniform rate more nearly harmonizes with the character of the banking process. The banking business is quite homogeneous. Technological differences, characteristic of industrial enterprise, are for the most part absent from banking operations. Credit is remarkably mobile and is but little hampered by political boundary lines or jurisdictional limits. Moreover, it is certainly to be hoped that the minor liberalizations of the national banking code with respect to branch bank expansion effected by the Banking Act of 1933 do not constitute the final position of Congress on this vital issue. If Congress does not see fit to nationalize the commercial banking business and thus promote the development of sound banking, it is to be expected that it will at least broaden the limits to branch banking conducted under federal charters. It is extremely doubtful whether even the rich resources of the United States can long support the dubious luxury of forty-nine banking systems. The authorization of a maximum uniform rate on national bank shares imposed under state authority harmonizes with probable future steps in the federalization of commercial banking. Taxes on branches can be allocated on a basis either of capital employed, or on deposits, or if preferable, a combination of both capital and deposits.

Again, the principle of a maximum uniform rate, once established, injects into the bank tax problem an element of flexibility through time which the existing methods do not to the same degree possess. It is not to be expected that the initially selected rate is inviolable. Rather it can be adjusted upward or downward whenever in the discretion of Congress changes are warranted on a showing of fact. Flexibility in the maximum rate is probably easier to obtain than flexibility in the methods of bank taxation.

Finally, the proscription of a maximum rate on national bank shares will give greater latitude to the several states in the taxation of other subjects. It frees the state tax system from the paralyzing restrictions of a permissive tax clause which would relate the rate on national banks to a considerable portion of the tax-paying public. Section 5219 as it now stands succeeds in relating the burden on banks to the taxes imposed on every important subject except public utilities and railroads. Nor is it possible to devise a permissive clause to protect the banks, on the one hand, and give ample latitude to the states, on the other, without involving a substantial portion of the entire tax system in the limitations with which Congress seeks to surround its federal agencies. It is submitted, therefore, that the taxes on national banks which some general property tax states might lose in the adoption of the proposed solution, which amounts incidentally would be but a very small fraction of their total revenue (less in fact than one per cent) would be more than offset by the greater latitude they would have both as to the method and degree of taxation of other subjects. Why involve practically the entire tax system of the state in a permissive tax clause relating to national banks if reasonably satisfactory revenues can be obtained from these institutions by the adoption of a maximum tax rate?

The objections to the proposal are obvious. Bankers in states now employing the excise or income tax methods will be opposed to a proposal which permits, though it does not compel, higher taxes. General property tax states will reluctantly yield the more productive rates which in a few instances they have still been able to enforce. It will also be contended that in practice the maximum rate will be employed against banks irrespective of the rates on other property, a contention which is not fully supported, however, by the history of bank taxation. The proposal may also encounter

objections from those who dislike the establishment of the principle of a maximum permissive state levy on any federal agency
or instrumentality.   It will be distasteful to those, principally
bankers and their organized spokesmen, who oppose all share
taxes on the ground that they are not contingent upon current
earnings.   Despite these objections, significant though they are,
the proposal offers a reasonable compromise solution to the present
impasse.

APPENDIX

SECTION 5219 UNITED STATES REVISED STATUTES, AS AMENDED

(U. S. C. Title 12. Sec. 548)

Sec. 5219. The legislature of each State may determine and direct, subject to the provisions of this section, the manner and place of taxing all shares of national banking associations located within its limits. The several States may (1) tax said shares, or (2) included dividends derived therefrom in the taxable income of an owner or holder thereof, or (3) tax such associations on their net income, or (4) according to or measured by their net income, provided the following conditions are complied with:

1. (a) The imposition by any State of any one of the above four forms of taxation shall be in lieu of the others, except as hereinafter provided in subdivision (c) of this clause.

(b) In the case of a tax on said shares the tax imposed shall not be at a greater rate than is assessed upon other moneyed capital in the hands of individual citizens of such State coming into competition with the business of national banks: *Provided,* That bonds, notes, or other evidences of indebtedness in the hands of individual citizens not employed or engaged in the banking or investment business and representing merely personal investments not made in competition with such business, shall not be deemed moneyed capital within the meaning of this section.

(c) In case of a tax on or according to or measured by the net income of an association, the taxing State, may, except in case of a tax on net income, include the entire net income received from all sources, but the rate shall not be higher than the rate assessed upon other financial corporations nor higher than the highest of the rates assessed by the taxing State upon mercantile, manufacturing, and business corporations doing business within its limits: *Provided, however,* That a State which imposes a tax on or according to or measured by the net income of, or a franchise or excise tax on, financial, mercantile, manufacturing, and business corporations organized under its own laws or laws of other States, and also imposes a tax upon the

[132]

income of individuals, may include in such individual income dividends from national banking associations located within the State on condition that it also includes dividends from domestic corporations and may likewise include dividends from national banking associations located without the State on condition that it also includes dividends from foreign corporations, but at no higher rate than is imposed on dividends from such other corporations.

(d) In case the dividends derived from the said shares are taxed, the tax shall not be at a greater rate than is assessed upon the net income from other moneyed capital.

2. The shares of any national banking association owned by non-residents of any State, shall be taxed by the taxing district or by the State where the association is located and not elsewhere; and such association shall make return of such shares and pay the tax thereon as agent of such nonresident shareholders.

3. Nothing herein shall be construed to exempt the real property of associations from taxation in any State or in any subdivision thereof, to the same extent, according to its value, as other real property is taxed.

4. The provisions of Section 5219 of the Revised Statutes of the United States as heretofore in force shall not prevent the legalizing, ratifying, or confirming by the States of any tax heretofore paid, levied, or assessed upon the shares of national banks, or the collecting thereof, to the extent that such tax would be valid under said section.

www.ingramcontent.com/pod-product-compliance
Lightning Source LLC
Chambersburg PA
CBHW021602210326
41599CB00010B/561